ARCHITECTURAL DIGEST
Autobiography of a Magazine 1920-2010

THE
ARCHITECTURAL
DIGEST

ARCHITECTURAL DIGEST
Autobiography of a Magazine 1920-2010

PAIGE RENSE

RIZZOLI
NEW YORK

New York · Paris · London · Milan

CONTENTS

Foreword by Mario Buatta 6
Preface 8

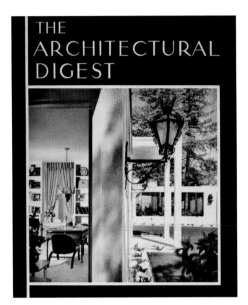

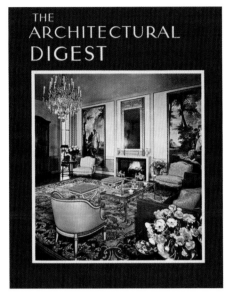

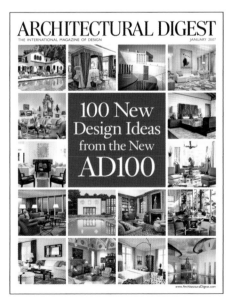

FOREWORD

s a young man, I was surrounded by a family devoted to the worlds of architecture and interior decoration. My maternal grandfather and his architect-trained son were talented in building private homes for family and friends. They buried themselves in monographs of architects past and present to incorporate ideas into their own work. I looked over their shoulders and took notes. I decided to follow their careers and entered Cooper Union for architecture studies. I didn't last long, as I found the math and the school's intention to flood us with the new tomorrow of contemporary studies uninspiring. It was then that I realized I had no interest in where pipes should be placed. My interest was where the furniture and art landed. Another inspiration was my aunt Mary. She was a follower of all the shelter magazines in her day and redecorated her house according to the whims of the editors. At one point, it resembled a decorator show house of the coming 1970s!

I was also fascinated by my first trip to England, where I discovered the legendary John Fowler and Nancy Lancaster. I knew then that I had found myself! Like Aunt Mary, I too became especially interested in publications of the day—one that stood out was a West Coast quarterly named *Architectural Digest*. I was mesmerized by the designs they published. In 1970 Paige Rense joined the magazine, playing up international interior decoration and architecture. She turned it into a bible for decorators and architects. For forty years, she produced an amazing mix of talent from the world over, filling upwards of 400 pages an issue. She also delivered interviews with major architects and people in related fields to educate readers about the who, what and where of design. *Architectural Digest* was tops in its field. *Bravissima* to Paige!

—*Mario Buatta*

ABOVE: The master bedroom of a house in Virginia designed by Mario Buatta. December 2003.
PAGES 2-3: The entrance to a Beverly Hills home designed by Edward F. White. Fall 1963.

A portrait of Paige Rense taken by Kenneth Noland.

PREFACE

ur focus when putting this book together was nothing less than the entire world. At *Architectural Digest*, I was not interested in trends and certainly not in fads. I preferred to speak of style, which is really a way of seeing and living creatively in the world. In 1970, after joining a three-person editorial staff, it seemed essential that *Architectural Digest*, founded in 1920, become well known nationally and, not incidentally, internationally, to survive in the competitive world of publishing. I wanted people to talk about the magazine, and one way to create talk was to feature homes of Hollywood celebrities and international style setters. And it worked.

In the November-December 1975 issue of *Architectural Digest*, I tackled the subject of criticism in my column. "The basic point is that none of us will ever like everything presented in any publication," I wrote. "It is our objective to report the most interesting designs wherever we find them." As I stated above, I was not interested in trends and certainly not fads. In my forty years as editor of the magazine, that is precisely what I attempted to do: report. I did not send producers, stylists or even editors when the magazine photographed a residence.

That mission inspired a number of innovative issues, among them the "AD100," "Before & After" and others, including "Hollywood at Home," "Country Houses," "Architecture," "Exotic Homes Around the World" and "Designers' Own Homes," not to mention international editions of the magazine in more than five countries and over a dozen books. We took our readers into the homes of celebrities, presidents, kings and queens, and artists, and featured the work of some of the finest writers of their generation, along with unforgettable images by the best photographers. It's safe to say that *Architectural Digest* launched the careers of countless architects and interior designers around the world in the process.

—*Paige Rense*

THE ARCHITECTURAL DIGEST

CHAPTER ONE

1920-1962

If Only It Could Have Been in Color

A Bel-Air residence shot by famed architectural photographer
Julius Shulman adorned the cover of the Spring 1962 issue.

In the late 1910s, Southern California was a land of dreams. Its orchards, its clean air and its pioneer spirit all lured people in search of something greater, initiating a period of dynamic economic growth and expansion that was reflected in the magnificent architecture springing up throughout the region. It was also the dawning of the Hollywood film industry, and the Art Deco movement was about to whet a worldwide appetite for design. For Tennessee native John C. Brasfield, who had enjoyed successful careers in importing and advertising, in New York and Illinois respectively, trips to California proved too great a siren song: he moved his family to Los Angeles. Impressed by Southern California's myriad styles of historically inspired architecture, Brasfield had an idea. He would publish an architectural digest that would show the innovative work of the architects that were building— and defining—California style.

With its inaugural issue in 1920, The Architectural Digest became the West Coast's pictorial review. Published in downtown L.A. by a handful of staff, the quarterly functioned as

ABOVE AND RIGHT: Grauman's Chinese Theatre in Hollywood, circa 1928.

Grauman's Chinese Theatre, Hollywood—Meyer & Holler, Inc., Architecture, Engineering and Construction

South Terrace

Photo, Hiller

Residence of Mr. and Mrs. E. L. Doheny, Jr., Beverly Hills—Gordon B. Kaufmann, Architect

Paul G. Thiene, Landscape Architect

a lavishly illustrated trade journal with large-format, black-and-white photos and limited text—essentially captions that credited architects, builders and suppliers. Brasfield, who used the highest-quality paper available to lend a feeling of luxury, focused on residential architecture, but he also showed commercial buildings like department stores and movie theaters. From its inception, the magazine drew big-name architects, among them Wallace Neff and Gordon Kaufmann, and it wasn't long before Hollywood came calling. In 1927 the magazine published the

Beverly Hills home of silent-film comedian Buster Keaton, followed by celebrity homes like Pickfair, built by Neff for Mary Pickford and Douglas Fairbanks (the house was razed in the early 1980s), and the Bel-Air home of movie mogul Louis B. Mayer. Each issue covered the full range of popular architectural styles, from Spanish Colonial to Tudor and Georgian revivals, and occasionally more modernist designs. The projects kept coming and the readership grew—Brasfield was onto something.

In just ten years The Architectural Digest became synonymous with success. The 1930s issues were celebrity-packed (Hollywood stars like Norma Shearer were happy to publish their homes, even without their portraits) and by the 1940s, the magazine included homes from across the United States. To meet the changing demands of readers' interests, Brasfield shifted the magazine's focus to interiors. There were early decorators like

LEFT: The Beverly Hills residence of Mr. and Mrs. E. L. Doheny, Jr., designed by architect Gordon Kaufmann, circa 1930. ABOVE: Villa del Sol d'Oro in Sierra Madre, California, by architect Wallace Neff, circa 1928.

TOP: The entrance hall of Greenacres, the Beverly Hills home of actor Harold Lloyd, circa early 1930s. BOTTOM: The galleria. RIGHT: Lloyd's living room as it appeared in the magazine.

Elsie de Wolfe, Frances Elkins, Nancy Lancaster and Dorothy Draper, who designed for the upper echelons of society, but the postwar era saw a booming middle class, which also meant a booming housing market. Suddenly, it wasn't just affluent families that needed help decorating their homes. Demand for professional decorators soared, as did the circulation of magazines like House Beautiful and House & Garden, which offered practical advice to readers. Brasfield, however, continued to show high-end homes, offering his readers inspiration rather than instruction.

During the 1950s features became more informative, with occasional texts and captions that identified noteworthy items like artworks. What remained unchanged was the presence of celebrity features and the quality of the projects shown, be it a modernist design by Paul László or a Georgian Revival by Paul R. Williams. Some were even photographed by then-little-known photographers like Julius Shulman. The magazine's freedom to publish only what it wanted to publish helped define its role as a leading resource for the best in design. The 1954 spring issue states in the front pages: "Issued every four to six months, depending on desirable material available." Brasfield's passion was genuine.

When he died in September 1962 at the age of eighty-two, he left his firm, the John C. Brasfield Publishing Company, to his daughter, Sally. Shortly thereafter, the company was purchased by Brasfield's twenty-one-year-old grandson, Cleon T. "Bud" Knapp, for $65,000. Knapp had worked at the magazine since he was in high school and knew not only how it worked but also what it needed to stay relevant. With a new name, Knapp Communications Corporation, and with his mother on the masthead as an associate, Knapp initiated a series of changes to contemporize the magazine and broaden its appeal, all while remaining true to his grandfather's vision of a largely pictorial presentation of luxury homes.

THE EARLY YEARS

Once upon a time, *Architectural Digest* was a black-and-white publicity showcase for any furniture store or decorator who could provide—gratis—photographs of

Living Room

Photo, Clark

Residence of Mr. and Mrs. Harold Lloyd, Beverly Hills — Webber and Spaulding, Architects

their work, especially after buying a page or so of advertising. Bud Knapp once told me it was called "the whore of the West." It was not on newsstands at that point and Bud told me circulation never came near even 50,000, but he believed, against all odds, that the magazine had a future. He once said that he was convinced that, unlike magazines that were going after younger audiences, there was a niche for affluent homeowners who wanted to see elegant, glamorous décor. The only notable publishers in Southern California at that time were Petersen Publishing, which primarily focused on cars, and a teen magazine. A few

national titles had West Coast offices, but New York City was, as it is now, the center of magazine publishing. The West Coast was of little editorial interest—national magazines were only interested in Hollywood movies and their stars. *House Beautiful* and *House & Garden* ruled what advertising people called shelter books. That's the way it was.

BUILDING CALIFORNIA STYLE

Architects like Wallace Neff, Gordon Kaufmann, Gerard Colcord, George Washington Smith (who "owned" Santa Barbara) and John Byers reigned over the earliest issues. The pages were filled with sepia photographs of mixed Spanish-Moorish-Mediterranean houses of real interest, but the accompanying captions were usually five- or six-inch lists of credits—cement stairways, gas heaters, plastering, plumbing and, my favorite, "Trees: F. Pearl." Some of the early

LEFT: The dining area of Mr. and Mrs. Edward L. Alperson's home in Beverly Hills, with interiors by Gladys Belzer, circa 1953. ABOVE: Actor Gregory Peck's house in Los Angeles's Pacific Palisades neighborhood, circa 1951.

issues even included lengthy essays on water heaters and the wonders of gypsum. There were sometimes real surprises too, like the old Pig 'n Whistle restaurant in Hollywood and a special ten-page section on the Elks lodge in San Francisco that showed a large mural depicting two barely clothed men embracing—X-rated architecture! There were movie palaces like the Egyptian Theatre and Grauman's Chinese Theatre, where I worked as a summer usherette—no cineplexes, those. And there were mansions with wishing wells. Did the owners wish for more? Almost all of the early Mediterranean-inspired houses were dark. The furniture was dark and its placement a model of discomfort.

One house showed a very large fireplace with yards of fringe hanging under the mantel, just inches above the flames. No interior designers were ever mentioned—that would change.

Non-residential issues were published too, showing office buildings, clubs, churches, banks, de-

ABOVE: The entertainment room in the Encino, California, home of John Wayne. Fall 1960
RIGHT, ABOVE: The Beverly Hills residence of Doris Day and husband Martin Melcher, circa 1959. RIGHT, BELOW: The couple's "Cozy Room."

partment stores and, of course, theaters. The magazine even published a mausoleum in Santa Barbara. By 1930 the quarterly editions cost $7.50, though two of the four were really just stapled pamphlets. Well, John C. Brasfield was ahead of us. He offered back then what is now called a blow-in card (you know, those "subscribe and save $75" cards that fall out of an issue). His paper insert offered substantial savings and went into great detail. For example, you could check your preferences for Homes, Out-of-Print or All Types. Personally, I find "out-of-print" irresistible.

LEFT: The entryway of Clark Gable's residence in Palm Springs, California.
ABOVE: The living room. Spring 1960

HOLLYWOOD'S STARRING ROLE

From its earliest days, movie stars were an important part of the magazine. Pickfair, the famous residence of Mary Pickford and Douglas Fairbanks, ran in one early issue but was shown on two pages. Why only two? We will never know. One 1930 issue opened with quite a different feature: the legendary estate of silent film star Harold Lloyd in Beverly Hills on twelve pages. If only it were in color. Landscape architect A.E. Hanson deserved his name on a marquee. The architects were Webber & Spaulding, who also built Irene Dunne's house. Just a few years later, in 1936, *The Architectural Digest* published a celebrity-packed issue involving many good California architects, all of whom gave photographs of their work to the magazine. Celebri-

Living Room   Photographed by Maynard L. Parker

Residence of MR. and MRS. JERRY LEWIS   Bel-Air, California

Interior Design by DONNA FLANAGIN of RALPH POTTER AND ASSOCIATES
Custom Carpeting by SHELLEY'S FLOOR COVERINGS INC
Custom Covered Upholstery Designed by DONNA FLANAGIN and Executed by
CLIFFORD RADFORD and SONS in Red, Orange and Pink Quilted Print
Hanging Lamp Over Grand Piano Designed by DONNA FLANAGIN of
RALPH POTTER AND ASSOCIATES

Red Lacquer Custom End Tables—Antique White Cocktail Table—White Alabaster Custom Lamps

ties and their architects included Constance Bennett and James E. Dolena; David O. Selznick and Roland Coate; and Dick Powell with Richard Frederick King. Cliff May's own home was featured in the issue. Floor plans were included for those who might want to replicate homes of the stars.

Visits to entertainers' homes became more personal over the years, like Mr. and Mrs. Jerry Lewis, who led the Fall 1961 issue. Their home in Bel-Air was a traditional two-story shingled house. Above the fireplace in the living room—laid with acres of carpeting—hung an oil portrait of the Lewises and their five sons. The room, which was immense and photographed from four angles, included a movie screen lowered for viewing of, it was said, Jerry Lewis movies. Why not? In his study was something else I had never seen before: photographs under a clear plastic floor pad. The bedroom was, the caption stated, mostly lavender, a color some psychologists believe is most conducive to romance. Well, there *were* five children in that portrait.

A NEW DIRECTION

Throughout the 1940s the issues showed houses by residential architects who would become blue chips of the west side of Los Angeles. It was still called *The Architectural Digest*, and there was still no masthead and no clear date on the issues, just volume numbers. The magazine was, however, beginning to credit interior designers. One issue featured two homes by architect James E. Dolena—one in Bel-Air and one in Brentwood Park—both with interiors by the great T.H. Robsjohn-Gibbings. Both homes got unprecedented ten-page spreads. Robsjohn-Gibbings's interiors were traditional, with carved moldings, high ceilings, built-in breakfronts, subtle carpeting, light colors and an overall look of comfortable formality. And they often had glamorous touches, like satin-covered beds and slipper chairs worthy of Jean Harlow.

Gibby, as he was known, would sometimes call me from his home in Athens, Greece, to just catch up with design-world gossip. He always had more time than I did, so he must have had a call list that he activated when he was bored, although it is difficult to imagine Gibby bored. He was witty and charming, as attested by

LEFT: Jerry Lewis's Bel-Air living room as it appeared in the Fall 1961 issue. ABOVE: The family room in Mr. and Mrs. Marvin Wilson's Encino residence. Fall 1960

several small books he wrote. If he was displeased with someone, his words cut one's head off as effectively as a well-honed blade. You didn't know what had happened until your head was rolling on the floor.

DESIGNERS ON THE RISE

The role of interior designers began to take on even greater importance by the late 1940s, not only in their residential projects but also in the lives of their clients. I am reminded of an evening at the Santa Barbara home of Joan Perry, widow of Columbia Pictures president Harry Cohn. She gave a party outdoors and pointed out to a visitor (me) a flame bursting from the ground on a small rise. "That used to be a barbecue pit," she told me. "But after my decorator, Arthur Elrod, died, I converted it to an eternal flame in his hon-

ABOVE: The Palm Springs residence of Mr. and Mrs. Thomas B. Davis, with interiors by T.H. Robsjohn-Gibbings. RIGHT: The family room. A series of panels behind the game table enclosed a stereo, a television and a small portable piano. Furniture throughout was designed and custom made by Robsjohn-Gibbings. Summer 1961

or." The field of interior design also saw an increase in female decorators, whose work began appearing in the magazine's pages. Just a few were Adele Faulkner, the first woman to be named a fellow by the American Society of Interior Designers, and Viola Bogue, who did Gregory Peck's home in the early 1950s.

I once met Mr. Peck at a dinner in Beverly Hills given by a titled lady whose name is lost from my memory. Mr. Peck was seated on my right. What would we talk about? Inspiration saved me. "Did you do a great deal of research for your role as General MacArthur?" He did. He replied through three courses. After the other guests had retired to the living room for coffee, he continued. At last, his beautiful wife, Veronique (a first-rate poker player), appeared and took him to the others. I hadn't told him that General MacArthur's widow, Jean, a friend of mine, couldn't bear to see the movie.

Hollywood and the design world also began to intertwine more closely. There was actress-turned-decorator Barbara Barondess MacLean, who decorated Jennifer Jones's home, and Gladys Belzer, Loretta Young's mother, who was loved but also the scourge of decorator showrooms. She was given to throwing her arms about as she talked, swinging a large handbag as she walked among breakable accessories, many antique. "She's here!" became a warning cry announcing her approach.

ADVERTISERS—OF ALL SORTS

The early issues featured ads in the back pages, usually for a variety of building materials. "The Construction of Your Floors Is Worthy of Serious Consideration" and "Why I Install Electric Heating in My Homes" by Cliff May, a good architect generally considered the father of the California ranch house. In one issue, May ran a half-page ad letting us know that his work was featured in *The Architectural Digest* in 1934, 1935 and 1936. Very desirable. Coincidentally, there was always a two-page advertisement for Cannell & Chaffin, a furniture store in downtown Los Angeles. Other early advertisers included the Pomona Tile Manufacturing Company and even a Ford service center and a Texaco gas station. Looking through these old issues, one ad brings on an attack of nostalgia: Rolling Hills Country Homes. "Five acres for the price of a city lot." It gets

better. A ranch-style home, four acres, barn, corral and orchard for $12,000. Before freeways. You just roll along on a boulevard and there you are. "Only 40 minutes from downtown Los Angeles."

A NEW LOOK

Throughout the 1950s and into the 1960s, there were still no headlines defining the features and only captions revealed the names of the residents, architects and designers. Texts were few. Most houses continued to be covered in very short features, often only a few pages. Mr. and Mrs. Max Factor. Mr. and Mrs. Lawrence Welk. And-a-one-and-a-two. And that's it. Two pages.

The issues were primarily filled with California interiors, with a dash of Texas and Florida, and everything looked very much alike—it was an era of gold-veined mirrors and acres of shag. You might call it midcentury without the great designs of that period. Hollywood figures appeared regularly—John Wayne in Newport Beach, Doris Day and Eartha Kitt in Beverly Hills, Clark Gable in Palm Springs—but changes were starting to be seen. Even more improvements to paper stock. Better photo reproduction. Better layouts. Interior design seemed cleaner, more sophisticated. Well, maybe.

In 1960 we see our first television set, right out there, naked. New York decorator Joe Braswell once told me, "Security is exposing your television set." Of course, today they are not only exposed, they dominate. And in 1962 *The Architectural Digest* paid its first visit to the White House. We published the Diplomatic Reception Room, with its Zuber wallpaper panels from the "Views of North America" series and its portrait of Dolley Madison over the fireplace. It was the redesign of Jacqueline Kennedy and the National Society of Interior Designers, then headed by Edward F. White, though neither he nor the First Lady were mentioned in the credits. As I said, if only it could have been printed in color! But that wouldn't come for another few years.

RIGHT, ABOVE AND BELOW: The Diplomatic Reception Room of the White House, redecorated by First Lady Jacqueline Kennedy and the National Society of Interior Designers. Spring 1962

THE
ARCHITECTURAL
DIGEST

CHAPTER TWO

1962-1971

A Calling Card for Architects and Designers

The living room of a Beverly Hills home designed by William L. Chidester appeared on the cover of the Winter 1965 issue.

In the years immediately following his grandfather's passing, Bud Knapp set about making significant changes to the magazine and realized he needed someone to oversee editorial content. In 1964 he hired Dallas-based decorator Bradley Little to serve as editor and to bridge the growing readerships of design professionals and design enthusiasts. It was a period that also saw the advent of color features (the first color cover appeared that year) and the expansion of the masthead to include advertising and circulation directors and subscription and business managers. It was the era of Madison Avenue ad men, and the magazine experienced exponential growth with more focused advertising. It even published its first "advertorial" (an advertisement produced like an editorial feature)—eighteen pages called "The World of Wallpaper."

Throughout the 1960s The Architectural Digest remained unencumbered by corporate direction and, perhaps without recognizing it at the time, was an early advocate for equality—it published whomever it chose, regardless of race, gender or sexual orientation. Celebrity figures Rita Hayworth, Mickey Rooney, Sonny and Cher, June Allyson, and Johnny Mathis were featured alongside architects and designers who were becoming celebrities in their own right: John Elgin Woolf, John Lautner, Buff & Hensman, Tony Duquette, Arthur Elrod, Jack Lionel Warner and McMillen Inc., the design firm that gave rise to Albert Hadley and Mark Hampton. Architects and designers especially appreciated the value of the magazine's editorials—publication meant their telephones rang with commissions. And while homes remained the focus of the issues, the magazine still included well-designed commercial spaces and new concepts, like the 1967 Pasadena Showcase House.

The magazine also began to expand its scope, showing a wider range of interior styles. Knapp wrote about the changes in his Winter 1967 publisher's letter: "I hope you will be pleased with the issue's balance and find an abundance of new ideas— never before thought of or seen." But there were challenges amid the successes. Knapp once recalled a failed promotion drive in 1968 that left the magazine in debt to the printer to the tune of about $100,000. "Counterintuitively," he said, "we charged more on the newsstands, switched to high-quality stock paper and did not discount subscriptions. In a sense, subscribers financed our growth, creating a liability that made our bankers cringe. But we won the game." In the end, it was readers' satisfaction that ensured the magazine's survival, and, by 1969, that satisfaction was reflected in dedicated advertising offices in Detroit and New York City. The big time was on the horizon.

While the 1960s saw smart and timely changes, it was the 1970s that inaugurated major innovations. In 1970 Knapp hired his first art director and brought on Paige Rense as associate editor. The first year of the decade was marked by a bold new look, which included the now signature white-bordered cover and color advertisements. Editorial content also found its voice. Major features included the legendary Paris hotel Le Bristol, "Vincent Price...on Art" (Price would later become a contributor) and Russia's famed Peterhof Palace. Readers also enjoyed an exclusive look at President Nixon's family compound in Southern California—the first of many political families to be featured in the magazine. In his publisher's letter, Knapp announced that the magazine would be published six times a year and delivered in protective mailers to ensure copies arrived in pristine condition. The quality of these exceptionally produced issues was manifested in the price: $17.25 per year (the

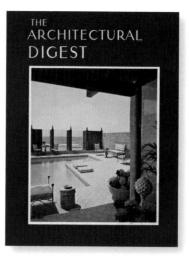

Don Loper's Bel-Air house. Spring 1965

equivalent of more than $100 today). So influential were the fea-
tures that the 1974 cover story on Dinah Shore's Beverly Hills home
designed by Val Arnold caused the red floral fabric he selected for
her garden room to sell out. The magazine's subhead, which had
changed over the years, was now "The Connoisseur's Magazine of
Fine Interior Design." Architectural Digest *(it was around*
this time that "The" was dropped from its name) was carving its
own niche in the magazine industry.

A NEW IDENTITY

In the Fall 1967 issue, the Editor's Note focused on the role *The Architectural Digest* played in emphasizing the importance of home and on connecting homeowners with designers and architects. Beyond the fantasy of being invited into incredible private homes, there was a practical aspect to the magazine: it was a calling card for architects and designers.

"Never before has there been such a wide-spread interest in good design of the home and its furnishings. Our present economy provides more people with more luxury products than ever before—and more leisure time in which to enjoy them. Spending more time in our homes, we are more conscious of their planning, comfort and appearance. Whether your tastes run to the exotic or the functional, there is a designer who can satisfy your needs within a reasonable prescribed budget. To be a good residential designer calls for many special qualifications; he must be a psychologist to interpret the needs of his clients, an advisor to guide them, and a

broker to see that their investments are sound; all these things must be in addition to having an artistic talent for creativity and an understanding of the personal needs of others. Whether it be an architect or a decorator you are hiring, choosing the right one for your needs is of utmost importance. Probably the most important thing is to find a designer who understands your way of living. This is necessary for him to be able to create workable and aesthetically pleasing backgrounds that are right for you. He has to be someone with whom you can communicate and have an open exchange of ideas. Word of mouth is quite often responsible for the client and the designer finding each other. Another method is to follow publications such as *The Architectural Digest* to see which designer's work most closely approximates your tastes and desires."

MY CAREER BEGINS

My name first appeared on the masthead of the "Fiftieth Anniversary" issue, November–December 1970, along with the first graphic director's name. We started on the same day. He was the first in a series. It was the beginning for the first writer, me. What were my qualifications? Few. This is how it came about.

One day a friend of mine on the staff of *Women's Wear Daily*, Hector Arce, told me that a magazine called *Architectural Digest* wanted a writer. I replied, "I don't know anything about architecture." He said, "It won't matter." I added, "My only magazine experience was at Petersen Publishing, you know—cars, skin-diving,

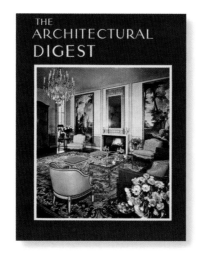

The master bath of actress Dana Wynter's Bel-Air residence. Winter 1965 FOLLOWING PAGES: Designer Michael Greer's New York City apartment. Winter 1965

Hollywood fashion." Again, Hector said, "It won't matter." I called, made an appointment with owner Cleon T. "Bud" Knapp and, several days later, went to the *Architectural Digest* offices near Bullock's Wilshire department store in Los Angeles.

He was younger than I expected. Somehow I expected a man named Cleon to be doddering. We chatted briefly, and then he asked me, "What would you do with the magazine to make it better?" I wanted to say, "I couldn't make it any worse." Instead, I said, "It could be akin to several European magazines, *Réalités* and *Connaissance des Arts*. Why not a beautiful magazine about interior decorating and how it all happens?" He nodded. (Later I learned that the magazine was not profitable enough to afford full-color printing.)

I was living in Marina del Rey with my first husband, Arthur Rense, a sportswriter for one of three major Los Angeles newspapers (now there is only one) and our cat, Bobby. Arthur was very encouraging about my work. We had met when we were both hired by Petersen Publishing to work for a startup magazine called *Water World*. (I'd previously been a record librarian, so my junior-high typing lessons paid off.) There were three of us—an editor, Arthur as managing editor, and me. My first reporting assignment took place on a beach in La Jolla, California, interviewing members of a skin-diving club called the Bottom Scratchers. I knew nothing about skin diving, so I just asked a lot of dumb questions.

Pickfair Revisited
...One of the Most Famous Homes in this Country

Its famous garden façade, left, has served as a backdrop for countless photographs of celebrities from around the world.

A view of the Motorcourt Entrance, below, reveals the welcoming, almost festive air that persists about the house. Meticulously maintained grounds are perhaps more beautiful than ever before.

The RECEPTION HALL, right, has a parquetry floor laid in an hexagonal pattern. The house has many beautiful and rare things such as the painted Adam cabinet. Drapery fabric by Scalamandré.

PHOTOGRAPHED BY MAX ECKERT

After a few issues, Robert "Pete" Petersen decided to do a series of softcover books. He asked me to do a book about Hollywood fashions. Later I learned his interest in the subject matter was prompted by a barely known starlet he was dating. She was to be on the cover.

LEFT: A page from the Fall 1966 issue showing the garden façade and driveway to Pickfair, the celebrated Beverly Hills home of early movie stars Mary Pickford and Douglas Fairbanks. ABOVE: Pickford's portrait hung over the mantel in the paneled living room. The house was designed by Wallace Neff.

Surprise. *Water World* didn't last long. It drowned.

My work at Petersen led to marketing jobs with Cole of California and Viviane Woodard cosmetics, freelance writing for *Cosmopolitan* and a reporting job with a fashion trade magazine. I don't remember the title, but that's where I met Hector Arce, a major influence on my career.

At the time of my interview, Arthur was recovering in the hospital from vasectomy repair surgery. It was not successful, so we did not have children. Now I wonder if I could have been both mother and editor. Editing a magazine is beyond a full-time job. It is all you can think about. Looking back, I never minded

and the editors of women's fashion magazines.

When I showed up at work, I was given an office and met the editor, Bradley Little. He was very gentlemanly and asked what I wanted to do first. I told him I would like to start interviewing decorators. He said, "They don't want to be interviewed." Really? Everyone, except Salinger, wants to talk about himself. Could decorators be different? "Let me try." He agreed.

Later that day Bud Knapp's wife came into my little office and said, "Hello. I'm Bud's wife. The thing you should know about him is that he's a con man." On that happy note, my first day at *Architectural Digest* began. A few months later fate decided everything.

ODDMENTS

Interiors shown in the magazine during the 1960s were not without their flights of fancy, and certainly not without lots of crystal and baroque elements. There was an "almost" grand piano in one master bath in 1965—I can recall it to this day; the lavish restoration of a Louisiana antebellum plantation; and actress Gail Patrick's twenty-fifth-floor apartment in Honolulu, called "Hale Pumehana," meaning "House of Warm Affection." A high-rise apartment *named*. A plantation, yes. A mansion, yes. A house, yes. A high-rise apartment? Please, no. Also published was dress designer Don Loper's Bel-Air home, which featured a doormat lettered "Wipe ya feet." Don is probably most famous for creating the iconic banana-leaf wallpaper for the Beverly Hills Hotel, but at the time there was a more infamous story. Once, after a bit too much champagne, he was unable to find his house keys and climbed up toward a second-floor open window. He fell, impaling himself on an iron spike fence, an injury that led to his death.

There were other surprises in the issues too, like "Photographs courtesy of *House Beautiful*." A credit like that was unheard of even then. One shelter magazine

the eighty-hour workweek; I thrive on work and this was a great job. There just wasn't much time for marriage. It wasn't a well-balanced life, but I was happy, although eventually Arthur and I divorced.

I did not hear from Cleon for a month. When he did call, he said, "Hi, it's Bud. Can you start work next Monday?" Briefly, I wondered who the hell "Bud" was, but I had actually applied for only one job. (Well, two, but *Women's Wear Daily* had no interest in me. Hector called to say he was sorry the reporting job hadn't worked out and that his editor had hired a girl from *Delicatessen News*. I told him that was the unkindest cold cut of all. Hector called me the next day and said he had reported our conversation to his boss, who had replied, "I hired the wrong one.") My hiring at *Architectural Digest* was probably due, in good part, to the fact that the salary was so low. At the time, the only female editors of major magazines were Helen Gurley Brown

The house is a collection of unusual things, used in an unusual manner. There are imaginative wall treatments, different applications of fabrics and furs, and unexpected uses of color. Some of the things came from old San Francisco houses; others were collected all over the world. This eclectic mixture of illogical objects, in the creative hands of this "wizard of design", become seemingly logical and natural. The resulting house, while attractive and interesting, can be used as an object lesson to all — for here we see an exercise in some of the basic principles of design, imagination and creativity, essential ingredients if a house is to have individuality and personality.

In the MAIN LIVING ROOM, walls, ceiling, and mantel are marbleized in tones of blue. Rare Seventeenth century Chinese painted panels form an overmantel treatment. The height of the ceiling is emphasized by the full length mirror.

The end of the Living Room shows a venturous use of two Mexican straw tables and a modern coffee table of crushed abalone shell. The sofa has colorful pillows of bright Indian cottons. The bamboo blinds are lined with leopard.

publishing photographs credited to another shelter magazine? Something borrowed, something new. And in one early 1971 issue, we encounter a rare painting—large, abstract, neon effect, multiple colors. Shades of red dominate. But that is not what is unusual. No. It is its unique placement that stuns the eye. From its base above a sofa, it explodes up to the ceiling—and then does an Olympic athlete's backbend, pasting itself on the ceiling. The interior designer acknowledges that he himself "designed" it.

LIONS AND TIGERS AND BEARS!

What really jumps out at me now looking back at these early issues is the frequency of animal skins in the layouts—something I later stopped. The San Marino home of Otis Chandler, the publisher of the *Los Angeles Times*, featured two stuffed and mounted polar bears standing in attack position flanking a huge fireplace in the appropriately named Game Room. The photogra-

pher's assistant noticed that they had been shot in the back. There was another casualty in an Arthur Elrod–designed residence in Palm Springs—a tiger skin flattened under a coffee table. I find myself fantasizing that the tiger will leap to life, throw off the coffee table and eat the residents and their decorators. There was also an Aspen ski lodge with a zebra in its entrance hall. And then there was Valerian Rybar's design for Christina Onassis's Saint Moritz chalet. In the master

ABOVE: A spread from the Summer 1966 issue revealed the main living room of designer Tony Duquette's San Francisco residence. RIGHT: The dining room. FOLLOWING PAGES: The drawing and sitting rooms of Elizabeth Arden's beloved 12th-century Irish castle, with interiors by Tony Duquette. The designer furnished the retreat largely with French pieces from the 18th and early 19th centuries and completed the interiors just a few months prior to Arden's death in October 1966. Winter 1967

bedroom was a huge upholstered headboard and spread, stitched together with many, many skins of Canadian wolves. In my dreams, the wolves, like the aforementioned tiger, also come to life and eat the sleeping occupants, applauded by the zebra. I have always believed in the rights of animals and never liked seeing them used as decorative elements.

ABOVE: A metal sculpture by Charles Hinman was above the fireplace in the Northbrook, Illinois, home of designer and architect Richard Himmel. RIGHT: Two paintings by Frank Stella hung in the dining area of the Himmel residence. Spring 1969

PEOPLE ARE THE ISSUE

The 1960s marked the beginning of designers and other talented types wanting to publish their own homes in *The Architectural Digest*—something that would later lead to books and an annual issue devoted to the subject. Some of the first to be featured were interior designers William Pahlmann, Yves Vidal, William G. Gaylord, and legendary photographer and Oscar-winning costumer and art director Cecil Beaton. It also marked the beginning of recurring appearances by rising design stars like Arthur Elrod and Michael Greer.

Designers were becoming recognized for their personalities as much as their work, and many devel-

oped a fan following. When Elizabeth Arden needed to decorate her twelfth-century Irish castle, she chose the more-than-fanciful Tony Duquette. Tony was a charmer, and on any given weekday a circle of society ladies sat in his Los Angeles studio helping to make his jewelry. Once Doris Duke was part of the group; their pay was a jolly lunch. For Arden's castle, Tony showed remarkable restraint—until he just couldn't hold back any longer. One bedroom surprised with patterns everywhere: walls, windows, bedspread, bed curtains. And then even more curtains, all in red with green trim. Houseguests were known to complain of sleepless nights.

In 1970 actor Vincent Price penned a very long article written as if we were in his home listening to his beliefs about art, collecting and plants. The layout showed five paintings and many copper pots. It was personal, charming and perhaps excerpted from a book he authored. Later that year we also published the western White House in San Clemente, the winter home of President and Mrs. Richard Nixon. The Spanish-style home was decorated by Cannell & Chaffin, who followed Mrs. Nixon's wishes to create a home that expressed the First Family's preference for casual living. Incidentally, I have never understood why any First Lady is assumed to be an expert on decorating, art, architecture, large-scale formal entertaining, food, menus, china, silver, music and landscaping.

The magazine's pages were truly becoming the place to be seen. For a designer to be published in the

magazine, it was a personal certification. For the resident, it was a social one.

CHANGES AFOOT

In the early 1970s the cover's subtitle changed several times, from describing the magazine as "The Home as a Work of Art" to "The Quality Guide to Home Decorating Ideas." (In fact, one so-called circulation expert even suggested we change the title of the magazine from *Architectural Digest* to *Manor* to boost sales.) Publishing frequency increased from four to six issues per year, mailed in protective cardboard cartons, and issues were sold only in fine department stores, decorating studios, bookstores and on select newsstands.

Advertisements changed too: full-color advertising pages appeared in the front of the issues. Ads were no longer in the back of the bus.

There were lots of other big changes happening too: more Midwest and international features, a

PRECEDING PAGES: Interior designer Arthur Elrod's Palm Springs house, designed by architect John Lautner. The seating groups in the living room included pieces by Charles Hollis Jones and offered different views of the desert, mountains and the city below. The sofa, the curved bench and the Pierre Paulin ribbon chairs were upholstered with rust-colored stretch fabric by Jack Lenor Larsen. ABOVE AND RIGHT: The master bedroom. Near the fireplace wall, designed with illuminated bookcases, were Warren Platner easy chairs. Spring 1970

The DINING ROOM, right, reflects Mrs. Nixon's preference for French inspired styles. Soft lighting and subtle colors give the room an atmosphere of warmth and hospitality. Pale gold walls provide contrasting backgrounds for the colors of the oriental style rug and the bright blue velvet on the host chairs. Crystal chandelier is from Cannell & Chaffin Import Shop.

A BREAKFAST AREA, left, is furnished in the Italian Provincial style with a round table by Heritage and cane armchairs by Lobeline Furniture Co. Colors continue the scheme of the Living Room, repeating the rug and adding floral patterned draperies by Stroheim & Romann. Area rug from Sallee.

Throughout the house are numerous objects of personal significance — gifts from heads of state and souvenirs from trips to the Orient. Below left, a lacquered panel from Vietnam, an inlaid Chinese box, and items from Nepal. Below, a small lacquered chest from Korea inlaid with mother-of-pearl.

14

new typeface and headlines for every feature. Interiors, mostly traditional in style, began to run in color. Bradley wrote pages of lengthy captions and articles describing design. He had knowledge of decorating and was a master of the cliché, which may have been just right for a period when using a decorator was still not that common. Contemporary art became a greater focus too, especially in one Richard Himmel–designed house in Chicago. It was the first interior feature to highlight a major art collection on the walls: Morris Louis, Ellsworth Kelly, Kenneth Noland (may I add that I did not meet Kenneth, my late husband, until years later) and Frank Stella. Oddly, only Louis was mentioned in the captions.

A SPLASH OF HUMOR

I love a funny anecdote, and one of my favorites in looking back through the issues is the May-June 1971 story we published called "Swimming Pools Accent the Total Design." An entire feature devoted to pools—and some very particular homeowners! In it, the following story was recounted: "A well-known chronicler of what he termed Real Society once wrote about a lady who lived in a Florida villa back in the twenties. Madame liked to swim in her pool but didn't like to turn around. So, she took her butler to the beach where she swam while he walked along the shore, measuring the distance. Then the lady simply had her pool extended to the length she could comfortably swim—without turning around."

ABOVE: Pages from the Winter 1970 issue displayed the dining room, breakfast area and an array of personal objects in President and Mrs. Richard Nixon's private winter residence in San Clemente, California. RIGHT: The arched entrance to the Spanish-style home's large interior patio.

ABOVE: The grounds were landscaped to allow for dramatic views of the ocean.
OPPOSITE: The living room. The Nixons hired Cannell & Chaffin to design the interiors.

ABOVE: The pool area of Sonny and Cher's Bel-Air residence. Ron Wilson, who would go on to decorate a number of residences for Cher, designed the interiors for the Mediterranean-style home, which reflected Cher's love of antique furniture and Sonny's interest in period paintings and bronze sculptures. RIGHT: The dining room. Summer 1970

Sonny and Cher's master bedroom.
The carved-wood four-poster bed,
candelabra lamps and French provincial
desk gave the space a European feel.

Interior designer Joseph
Braswell created the interiors—
as well as the painting—for
the home of Mr. and Mrs.
Morton Rosenberg in New
Jersey. January-February 1971

ARCHITECTURAL DIGEST
THE CONNOISSEUR'S MAGAZINE OF FINE INTERIOR DESIGN

ABOVE AND RIGHT: Peterhof Palace near St. Petersburg, Russia. A summer home for Peter the Great, the palace was built in 1709; by 1722, nearly 300 acres of formal gardens and fountains had been added. The property, in ruins after World War II, underwent full restoration shortly thereafter. May-June 1971

ARCHITECTURAL DIGEST

THE INTERNATIONAL MAGAZINE OF FINE INTERIOR DESIGN

MARCH 1977 $2.95

CHAPTER THREE

1971-1981

Ignorance Was My Greatest Asset

The living room of a New York City apartment
designed by Jay Spectre. March 1977

*J*ust as Architectural Digest *began to chart its new course under Bradley Little, tragedy struck with his murder on April 9, 1971. Knapp credited Little with advancing the magazine's style and dedicated a page in the Spring issue to keeping Little's vision alive. In it he wrote,* "Bradley contributed to the Architectural Digest's *success—for which I am thankful—and built a standard I will, in turn, protect. I am deeply sad he will not be here to enjoy the fruits of his endeavor and help build the dreams we envisioned."*

After Little's death, Knapp interviewed replacement editors but none were found. With associate editor Paige Rense securing features and overseeing issues, the answer was right before him. Over the next several years Rense took the reins and shifted the editorial direction to reflect her idea of remaking Architectural Digest *in the tradition of European art magazines. It worked. By 1972 Rense had brought on foreign correspondents in London and Paris, and in 1973 she secured a ten-page feature on the home of Coco Chanel with a single phone call. She beat other titles in the chase to publish designer Angelo Donghia's own home, and she received a Letter to the Editor from none other than Joan Crawford, complimenting the magazine*

The living room of James Galanos's West Hollywood home melded 18th-century French furnishings with two small tables of his own design. Atop the 18th-century Dutch commode were Chinese *famille verte* vases and a neoclassical head. September-October 1971

West Hollywood, California. Every issue was a Who's Who in the world of international design and society: Mario Buatta, Val Arnold, Nancy Lancaster, Henri Samuel, Anthony Hail, François Catroux, Robert Metzger, Tom Britt, Steve Chase, Jay Spectre, Valerian Rybar, Michael Taylor, Philip Johnson, Horst and Valentine Lawford, Truman Capote, Julia Child, Marie-Hélène de Rothschild, Lee Radziwill, Yves Saint Laurent, Diana Vreeland, HRH Princess Margaret, Fred Astaire, Senator and Mrs. Edward Kennedy, Cher, Barbra Streisand, Malcolm Forbes, Woody Allen—the list of boldface names goes on and on. Rense also surprised readers with unexpected content, publishing features on Fabergé eggs, antique toys, dog portraits and even scientific instruments. Circulation skyrocketed from 50,000 to 200,000.

Playing on the magazine's success, Knapp founded the Knapp Press in 1977, under which Rense could publish collectible books that celebrated the incredible content found in the issues. Her first book, Celebrity Homes, was published that year, followed by additional titles and the Worlds of Architectural Digest series.

As the 1980s opened, the magazine was published nine times annually, with a circulation of 450,000 and issues rich with personalities like Roald Dahl, Paloma Picasso, James Caan and Brooke Astor. Demand for the magazine was worldwide, and Knapp responded by debuting international editions, first in Italy, in 1981, followed over the years by France, Germany and Spain, along with AD en Español, which was distributed in Latin America. One critic called AD "the most authoritative mirror of modern international lifestyle." But perhaps the biggest surprise arrived in December 1981, with an exclusive visit to the private quarters of the Reagan White House—a monumental feature that would shape the future of the magazine.

on its recent features on her friends William Haines and Earl Blackwell. Under Rense's editorship, which was cemented when Knapp officially promoted her to Editor-in-Chief in 1975, the magazine would reach its zenith.

Rense instituted key changes, like establishing relationships with well-known writers that added to the prestige of the magazine and helped secure exclusives. (One such being the private gardens of Chiang Kai-shek in Taipei, Taiwan, which was brought to AD by international journalist Irene Corbally Kuhn.) More contributors joined the masthead, including photographer Derry Moore, critic Russell Lynes and designer David Hicks. The stories became more personal, more intimate too, with recurring columns like "Artists' Dialogue" and "Architectural Digest Visits," the first of which was James Galanos in

ABOVE: On the piano were antiquities from Greece and China and a painting by William Brown. RIGHT: Galanos's bedroom doubled as his study and included his library and Directoire *bureau plat.* A dressing room adjoined the space.

A MURDER JUMP-STARTED MY CAREER

It was a typical morning at home. Coffee mug in hand. News on. A bulletin. "Bradley Little, editor of a local magazine, *Architectural Digest*, was shot and killed early this morning during a robbery. The shooting took place in the parking lot of Club John, a restaurant on La Cienega Boulevard. Police are looking for a white Cadillac with two men, one believed to be the shooter. Mr. Little's passenger was unhurt. If you have any information, please call..."

My phone rang. It was Bud, somewhere in the Northwest with his family. Had I heard? Could I get to the office right away and field any calls? Driving down Wilshire Boulevard, I recalled a mystery I had just read. A classic whodunit. Was Brad's murder a random robbery attempt? Were the two men waiting for anyone who had a few drinks and left the club? Was Brad their target? Why? Who profited from his death? Then I realized. Me. The editor was no more.

There was a job opening. I had something to gain. I was the logical suspect. Would the police think I had hired a hit man? My bank account would prove I couldn't afford one, and it was doubtful that hit men would accept credit cards.

I waited in the empty *AD* offices for a visit from the police. Gradually, the entire staff of five or six filtered in, eager to discuss this dramatic event. It wasn't that we didn't care about Brad, but no one really knew him well because he wasn't around very much. I had never even had a cup of coffee with him. His door was closed during the several hours he occupied his office. He was gentlemanly but his life seemed to be elsewhere.

ABOVE: A sitting area in Angelo Donghia's Connecticut home, April 1986. RIGHT: The downstairs living room of Donghia's Manhattan duplex expressed his utilitarian design philosophy with comfortable seating and functional accessories. November-December 1973

LEFT, ABOVE AND BELOW:
Donghia designed the upstairs
living room of his Manhattan
home with movable upholstered
pieces and called the space his
playroom. The Chinese
coromandel screen came from
the estate of Coco Chanel.
RIGHT: The mirrored
stairwell had a runner made
of Mexican serapes.

Finally, a radio station called for a comment. I relied on clichés. Yes, he was a great editor. He will be greatly missed. Loved by all who knew him. And so on. That was it. The police didn't appear. Didn't call. There was nothing for us to do but go back to work. So we did. Bud returned the next day and told me to take over the magazine until he found a new editor.

THE TURNING POINT

Several months, and endless interviews with potential prospects later, Bud casually announced that I was promoted to Editorial Director. No raise mentioned. He hung on to the Editor-in-Chief title, even though I had been doing that job from the first day I got there. Same work, new title. Nothing changed. Despite our grand titles, the staff was very small. Those early years, I wrote every issue myself. Bud basically sold advertising, leaving me to do editorial content with no restrictions.

My name first appeared on the masthead as Executive Editor in the July-August 1971 issue. It wasn't until the July-August 1975 issue that Bud officially handed over the Editor-in-Chief title to me.

I had been hired to change the magazine. I knew what it could be and how to get it there—a clear vision that never varied, though it took a long time to make it happen. One of the first things I did was start a network of international correspondents for worldwide, not just national, input. But the main thrust was improving the quality of the design material and hiring better writers and photographers. There had never been a photography budget, so designers had always paid for their own photographs, and for a time that worked. Our policy was that *AD* was a designers' forum, and if they controlled the pictures, their work would appear in the best light. But times were changing, and, as I explained to our financial fellow (yes, we at last had one), a photography budget was essential if the magazine was to grow and gain respect from its contributors. All the other magazines, after all, picked up that cost.

Since we were not on newsstands yet, we didn't have to lure readers with a provocative cover, and I was never asked to do anything to please advertisers. In fact, the editorial side had no idea who the advertisers were until we saw the printed issues. We presented our por-

Coco Chanel's living room in her private apartment at the House of Chanel in Paris. FOLLOWING PAGES: An alcove at one end of the living room served as a library. At the other end was the dining room. Chanel filled the entire space with European and Chinese antiques. January-February 1973

ABOVE: The living area of the Marina del Rey, California, home of art collectors Joan and Tomas del Amo, designed by Jay Steffy. Their collection included works by Helen Frankenthaler, Robert Rauschenberg, Peter Young and Laurence Dreiband. RIGHT: In the dining area were works by Kenneth Noland and Frank Stella. March-April 1973

tion, ads were inserted, and off to the printer it went. There were no rules about advertising versus editorial ratio. Our mission was simply to make every issue as wonderful as possible. As long as subscriptions grew, nobody bothered me. A few years later that would change as issues became more about profit. To this day, opening the January-February 1972 issue still leaves me breathless. A two-page spread advertising Rolls-Royce. It was official. *Architectural Digest* was a contender.

BEHIND THE PAGES

At the beginning, ignorance was my greatest asset. I was reasonably visual and frequented art galleries and antiques shops, decorating our homes from flea mar-

kets and auctions. We had little money, so I combed thrift shops for interesting pieces, used dress fabric for curtains and hung the walls with posters and prints. Books had always been my only education, so I knew when it came to design, I faced a very steep learning curve. Fortunately, decorators, architects and photog-

ABOVE: The living room of the McLean, Virginia, home of Senator and Mrs. Edward Kennedy, who worked with architect John Carl Warnecke and designers Keith Irvine and Thomas Fleming. RIGHT: Antiques included a Chippendale mantelpiece and an English desk used by the senator's father, Joseph Kennedy, while ambassador to the United Kingdom. September-October 1973

raphers loved to talk about their work and their worlds. What better education than learning about design from those who did it best?

At that point the respect factor for *AD* and me, especially among East Coast designers, was almost nil. I tried to convince people that the magazine had changed, but they were hesitant to appear in our pages, as I quickly learned after making a few phone calls to well-known decorators. Most had never heard of the magazine. I figured that if I could just snare one or two top designers, I could get them all, so I started with San Francisco. Bud had to approve any travel expenses, so I asked him if I could go and visit decora-

tors. He said, "Sure, Brad travels a lot and always comes back with photographs." I explained to Bud that those were photographs already shown by other magazines and that we had to be first in order to be taken seriously by decorators. "That's why I want to meet with them," I said, "and convince them that *Architectural Digest* will be an important showcase for their work." Hector had given me a list of the major designers in San Francisco, so I called for appointments, asking for a personal interview—my opening gambit. It worked. I told them I wanted decorators to be stars. Then I had to tell them that I did not have a budget for photography. Each interviewee assured me he would supply the photographer and send me pictures of work no other magazine had published. And they did.

It was decided that we would publish the interiors from San Francisco as they came in, although it was tempting to save them for a big "preview" issue. We just weren't going to have enough material to wait for the really good ones to come in. We received photographs, in due course, from Billy Gaylord, Tony

OPPOSITE: The entryway of Sonny and Cher Bono's next Los Angeles home. The couple called again on Ron Wilson to restore the 1936 house by architect Robert D. Farquhar. May-June 1974
ABOVE: The living room. Cher first visited the house when it belonged to Tony Curtis.

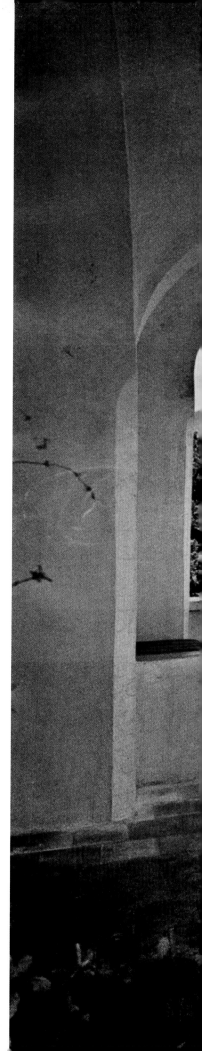

ABOVE, CLOCKWISE FROM TOP: A balcony at Gore
Vidal's Italian villa, La Rondinaia ("The
Swallow's Nest"), near Ravello. Vidal in the living
room, designed with Bill Willis. Wrought-iron
doors opened to the terrace. The villa was built in
1927 by Gladys Moore Vanderbilt, Countess
Széchenyi, and could only be reached by a
footpath. Famous guests included Greta Garbo.
RIGHT: Arches framed views of the Tyrrhenian
Sea and Vidal's terraced vineyards and orchards
below the house. November-December 1974

Hail, Val Arnold and a few others. I wanted the great Michael Taylor but I had to bide my time. There was no budget for writers, so I did it all—I even helped address subscriber copies.

San Francisco was a success, so I asked Bud if I could try New York. He agreed.

EXCLUSIVITY AND THE ALLURE OF *AD*

In 1973 I wrote to Angelo Donghia, a top New York decorator liked and respected by everyone in the business. We made a date for lunch at his favorite Italian restaurant and hit it off right away. He had just completed his new townhouse, and he told me, candidly, that all the magazines wanted to photograph it. He gave it to *Architectural Digest*, agreeing to have it photographed for the magazine. I had finally snagged someone who I knew could be the pied piper in getting top designers into *AD*. Donghia's clients included Barbara Walters, Diana Ross and Ralph Lauren—he was the man of the hour. Publishing his own home was the plum that everyone wanted. And *AD* got it. He was thrilled with the coverage. "*Architectural Digest* is the most important publication in the United States, Europe and probably South America," he said. "My French friends say that it is the hottest book in Paris. Rich people don't usually want to have their homes photographed but they all want to be in *AD*."

That was really the beginning. Once Angelo gave his seal of approval, other decorators—and even some architects—started paying attention and calling to tell me about their latest job. I asked them to supply scouting shots of their work, and they did.

Later that year we scored another coup. One day, driving to the office, I found myself wondering what had happened to the legendary, never-published, antiques-filled apartment of the late Coco Chanel. Using that old-fashioned instrument, the telephone, I called Paris journalist Mary Blume, who made a few calls and discovered that the Chanel apartment was exactly the same as it had been when she lived there. Voila! Our ten-page cover story. The apartment was incredible and, in terms of interior design, very influential. She was the first, I believe, to do mirrors-on-mirrors. Of course, she didn't really live there—only

The living room of Mario Buatta's Manhattan apartment, where he melded his signature chintz fabrics with yellow walls and a red Queen Anne secretary filled with his collection of antique ceramics. May-June 1974

entertained and napped. At night she walked to the Hôtel Ritz and slept in a very plain, small room. I'm always asked which, of all the rooms that I've seen, would I choose to live in? None—it's like wearing someone else's clothes. Though I could force myself to live in Coco Chanel's.

Architectural Digest always had to be first. I didn't care what came after. I confess to being excessively loyal to those designers in the very early years who gave me the work I very much needed. It was important to have the work before any other publication. The cover price was more expensive than other magazines in the field, and it seemed logical that readers could expect to find work in AD that they would not find in any other publication. During the Nixon years, we were the first to show the summer White House in San Clemente, as well as Ingrid Bergman's home in the South of France and Cecil Beaton's London and country houses.

THE NEW GUARD

The early 1970s were the beginning of a golden era for interior designers, and for the magazine too. I could see that the design world was changing, and so were AD's readers. Our audience was now younger and

above average in intelligence and style. Fashion designers were the superstars of the sixties but interior designers were the superstars of the seventies. What the leaders of Art Nouveau and Art Deco had done for their generations, the seventies designers—Michael Taylor, John Saladino, Diana Phipps, Michael de Santis, Robert Hutchinson, Stefano Mantovani, Jay Spectre, Melvin Dwork, Sally Sirkin Lewis—were doing for their own. They were masters of the nothing look—cleaning up the clutter, unafraid of space and believing in its intricacies. Whether placing a sofa, a simple basket or a priceless vase, they created a mood of serenity. In a chaotic world (we were in shock from Watergate at the time), the one thing we can control is our own home. The world may be spinning on its axis but our homes need not be. When humans feel out of control, they turn inwards, which I began to see in the design world. Architectural Digest merely reported what designers were doing.

ABOVE LEFT: A corner of the living room. ABOVE RIGHT: A Georgian-style bookcase in Buatta's bedroom held not only books but also a pair of Rouen pottery dogs. RIGHT: His Sheraton bed was draped in chintz and an antique quilt.

SISTER PUBLICATIONS

In 1975 Knapp purchased *Bon Appétit*, which had been a liquor store throwaway before it was purchased by Pillsbury. It had a circulation of 250,000, and I told Bud I could edit it, too. He agreed and I became Editor-in-Chief in 1976, a position I held until 1983. The only competition was *Gourmet*, with its long and complicated recipes, so I decided to make *BA* a food magazine for busy people. It was a formula that worked very well. There were other titles, too. Bud purchased *Geo U.S.A.*, which I edited from 1981 to 1985. It covered geography and travel but it never really found its identity, so it was eventually suspended. We also published *Home*, a magazine about home renovation, that was sold to Hachette in 1991.

THE LIFE OF AN EDITOR

I learned early on to never appear when or where photographers and writers were working. At first I tried going on shoots but it became clear that if I was there, the photographer was more concerned about what I thought the picture should be than what he did. He would want me to look in the viewfinder and check the shot, but that's his job, not mine. I decided that the best thing for everybody was to let photographers, along with writers, do what they do brilliantly, without me around.

Besides, I had my own busy schedule to keep. Many times I would get so overbooked and eat too much, starting with a breakfast appointment, then lunch, then tea, then cocktails and dinner. Of course I got hustled, but I must admit that I loved the attention. Why not? When it got overwhelming, I'd go off on a little retreat to Puerto Vallarta for three days and become an iguana.

ABOVE LEFT: Jay Spectre's Southampton, Long Island, home was a high-tech haven, with a stainless-steel cabinet that housed the indoor-outdoor sound system. ABOVE RIGHT: Spectre designed the house with architects Harry Bates and Dale Booher. March-April 1975 RIGHT: The window seat of Spectre's Manhattan living room, designed with Geoffrey Bradfield, ran on the cover of the March 1984 issue.

ABOVE: Diana Vreeland at home in Manhattan. RIGHT: The living room of the apartment she famously likened to "a garden in hell," designed with her friend Billy Baldwin. Vreeland stitched the needlepoint playing card pillows atop the sofa.

THE WHITE HOUSE

I first met Mr. and Mrs. Ronald Reagan in Los Angeles, pre–White House, at a dinner given by Betsy Bloomingdale. (Please remember that I knew such people were only interested in me because of my title at the magazine.) Ronald Reagan was charming. He may have been California's governor at the time. I don't recall, and dum-

LEFT: Stefano Mantovani's living room in Rome exuded the exotic spirit of French Romanticism, combined with Moroccan and Asian elements. ABOVE: The opposite end of the room featured Indian cotton curtains hand-painted with tigers. January–February 1976

my me never kept a journal. Their decorator was my friend Ted Graber. He had worked with William Haines, who had done the Reagans' house in the Pacific Palisades. After Reagan became president, I had to ask: "Ted, would the Reagans consider allowing *Architectural Digest* to publish their private quarters?" Well, yes. They would do it for their friend Ted, because it would be so important for him. *Whee!* It was a major coup for the magazine.

Ted invited me to lunch with him in the White House Mess. (I still have the menu.) We talked about which photographer to use. Ted had been thinking about it and looking through back issues. He liked the work of British photographer Derry Moore, a viscount. So did I, but I cautioned, "Shouldn't we use an American?" Ted said not necessarily. "After all, England is an

CLOCKWISE FROM TOP LEFT:
Truman Capote in his
Hamptons living room; an aerial
view of the two-story space;
Capote's writing table. RIGHT:
The home, built by a local
carpenter in 1962 to Capote's
specifications, reflected the
writer's desire for seclusion.
January-February 1976.
FOLLOWING PAGES: An antique
Japanese screen inspired Sally
Sirkin Lewis to paint cranes on
the gold-leafed wallpaper of her
Beverly Hills living room.
January-February 1976

ABOVE: The living room of Joan Crawford's last
Manhattan apartment reflected her longtime
friendship with William Haines, whose pieces she had
kept and had reupholstered. LEFT: The window end of
the room served as an office. RIGHT: A portrait of
the actress by Michaele Vollbracht. March-April 1976

ally, and Derry Moore has photographed American homes, too—some of the most beautiful pictures ever—and the Reagans left the decision to me." I pointed out that we didn't want to be arrested for treason.

Then we toured the private quarters to plan the photography. Graber had used some of the Reagans' furniture from their California residence, installed on Inauguration Day, to make them feel at home. He refreshed the quarters and used many pieces from the White House collection for the private apartments, yet there was also structural work to be done. Plumbing and electrical wiring was obsolete; draperies were falling apart; floors and doors had not been tended to since President Truman's day. Mrs. Reagan and the president declined to accept Congressional funds to refurbish their private quarters. Instead, Mrs. Reagan appealed for donations from the private sector, some of which were for just one dollar. "This house belongs to all Americans, and I want it to be something of which they can be proud," Nancy said. The private quarters were traditional; colorful but with restraint.

ABOVE: Yves Saint Laurent in the living room of his Paris home. RIGHT: The room included a 17th-century Chinese portrait and Eileen Gray's "Dragons" armchair. The Left Bank house was originally designed by Jean-Michel Frank and retained some original features, such as his fireplaces and copper window frames. September-October 1976

ABOVE: The library included a flock of Lalanne sheep and artworks by Léger, Picasso and Modigliani above a Le Corbusier–designed console. RIGHT: The Lalanne cocktail cart, custom designed for Saint Laurent in 1965, divided the room. Warhol's portraits of the designer were set atop the bookcase.

ABOVE: Fred Astaire in Beverly Hills. RIGHT: Astaire's living room opened directly to the pool and rose garden. FOLLOWING PAGES: Over the mantel was a painting by Max Gunther. The large painting at right is by Richard McKenzie, Astaire's son-in-law. March 1977

ABOVE: Michael Taylor's San Francisco home near the Presidio doubled as his office and showcased his talent for melding the raw and the refined. RIGHT: The living room was a harmonious interplay of pieces as divergent as the Louis XIV mirror and the Jean-Michel Frank granite table. December 1977

Derry was booked for the shoot. I was tempted to be present for it but felt I should stick with my policy of staying out of the way. The actual photography went smoothly. Only a slight hiccup when a member of the Reagan staff suggested that Derry get a hearing aid since he was not laughing at the president's jokes. The writer I sent was one I thought would be a comforting presence for the Reagans, Russell Lynes, a highly regarded essayist and a columnist for *AD*. The feature was a great success. Of course, with the exterior of the White House on the cover, the issue was huge on the newsstands, setting a sales record that stood for over a decade. All that attention created a big uptick in subscriptions.

CRAWFORD AND HAINES

William "Billy" Haines had been a popular movie star in the early days of film. Gay, he refused to give up or hide his partner, and moralist Louis B. Mayer fired him from MGM in 1933, ending his movie career. His great good fortune was a talent for interior design. He once recounted that when a client asked him, "What is your specialty?" he replied with, "We collect distinguished clients."

One of those distinguished clients was also his friend Joan Crawford. She had seen his home and asked him to design hers. He did, and his career as "decorator to the stars" began. It continued for many years. Shortly after Billy died, I published a feature on Joan's Manhattan apartment. We spoke often on the telephone, and when I mentioned that I had a tape of my interview with Billy, she asked me to please, please send it to her. I did. Joan was unfailingly gracious to me, a contradictory bit of information that might add to questions about the accuracy of her daughter's controversial book, *Mommie Dearest*. (Ted Graber, Billy's longtime assistant who took over the business after Billy's death, knew their clients well, and he told me that the book was quite accurate.)

Joan was certainly controlling and told our photographer, Richard Champion, how to shoot the interiors. After the shoot, she made him give her the film, saying that only she could be sure it would actually reach the magazine. It was received via FedEx two days

In the bedroom, Taylor paired a 17th-century Spanish bed with an 18th-century English *faux bois* table. Above the Dutch commode he placed a Matisse drawing and an 18th-century still life.

Paint-freshened Georgian paneling provides a crisp traditional background for Victorian artworks in the Sitting Room. LEFT: William Powell Frith's anecdotal 1881 canvas, *For Better, For Worse,* hangs above a warming fire. At left is Sir William Q. Orchardson's *The Queen of the Sword,* whose literary inspiration was Sir Walter Scott's *The Pirate.* Above the doorway is an unusual canvas by H. N. O'Neil, in which the artist replicated sensitive details from two of his narrative works. TOP: A 19th-century Pontypool lamp helps to illuminate J. J. Tissot's *'Good Bye'—On the Mersey.* ABOVE: This portrait by William Holman Hunt combines the characteristics of two women the artist loved.

112

113

later. She called me fairly often to check the story's progress. During one call, she mentioned that she didn't know what to do with all the clothes she no longer wore. I could only suggest that a museum would be happy to have them, without the least idea if that might be true. She continued calling. Finally, her last call reached me at the Golden Door spa, near San Diego, where I had checked in for the week. (I was probably the only magazine editor who actually paid the price of admission.) Joan was always charming.

At the Golden Door, I became friendly with another movie star, although one not as famous as Crawford. It was the somewhat eccentric Jean Arthur, who was getting in shape for a Broadway appearance as Peter Pan. When I first saw her at the spa, she was wading into the shallow end of the swimming pool wearing a swimsuit that looked like those long, knit, skirted suits from the 1800s, and she was carrying a parasol. Later, at breakfast on the fifth day of what now seemed like incarceration, she said that she wished she had a

car to get away for a drive. I had my car and volunteered. We set out without a destination in mind but came upon a supermarket. Jean said, "Let's stop. I've never been in one." We went in, and she seemed filled with wonder, roaming among the shelves. We left without buying anything. On the drive back, we saw farm animals. She called out, "Hello, cow!" Then, back to me, she asked, "Did you know my real name was Gladys Schmidt?" I didn't. We continued back to the spa without further greetings to cows. We published her Carmel home in the spring of 1976.

Designer Jay Steffy cast his clients as "F. Scott

ABOVE: A spread in the April 1979 issue showed Malcolm Forbes's London home, Old Battersea House. RIGHT: A portrait of Queen Victoria by J.H. Thompson hung above the fireplace in the Garden Room.

Fitzgerald people." At 28, he had been designing interiors for five years. Volatile, always candid, he was a brilliant photographer as well. "My interiors are portraits of the people," he said. He had a soaring, award-winning design career. He once placed ten Andy Warhol soup cans in my office, saying, "They belong here. They're yours." One day I returned from lunch and the wall was bare. No Warhols. "What happened, Jay?" "I sold them."

Valerian Rybar became a friend over the years. He was fiercely handsome and seemingly aloof and unapproachable. He was actually down to earth and witty. His family had moved to Paris from Yugoslavia, and his father promptly died. Valerian became, in his teens, the man of the family. From that blighted beginning, he became a friend and designer to wealthy internationals. His work was always bold. We were both in Venice at one time when he asked me to accompany him to the graves of his parents, buried on a small island in the lagoon. He brushed away tears. After a glamorous life of wealth, a house in Paris, a maisonette in Manhattan, he died, I was told, almost broke. If this were to be a morality tale, it's moral would be: "You can't live like your clients."

I met Diana Vreeland at a party in Manhattan. She said, "*Vogue* wants to photograph my apartment, but you can do it if you like." I liked. She described the primarily red apartment, which she designed with Billy Baldwin, as a "garden in hell." Another Vreeland quote as she toured our photographer through the rooms: "Anyone who could photograph this place would find the Sistine Chapel a cinch."

Many clients, after working with designers for one or two years or more, and sometimes with extensive travel, came to believe they were now friends and therefore, it was not in order to pay for their services. In that regard, I once accompanied Arthur Elrod to see a house in Palm Springs that he had almost completed. Usually I preferred to scout houses when the client was

For the entrance hall and living room of Cher's Malibu home, Ron Wilson used natural materials and Egyptian motifs, like the papyrus pattern on the tables. An antique Chinese wall hanging added an Asian influence. June 1979

ABOVE: Princess Margaret's Mustique retreat, designed by Oliver Messel. The property was the gift of her friend Colin Tennant when she married Lord Snowdon in 1960. RIGHT: The open living room epitomized Caribbean living and was decorated with bamboo pieces and Victorian plates. October 1979

away, but Arthur assured me I would not be trapped. In and out in twenty minutes. And it was so. His clients seemed fond of Arthur, so I asked him why they called him by his first name when he referred to them only as Mr. or Mrs. "It's simple," he said. "I only call them by their first names when the last check clears."

San Francisco-based John Dickinson was a very interesting person and a highly regarded designer. His furniture is now treasured by collectors. He once showed me shelves of carved wood figures that looked to be African but were covered in white lacquer. "Tell me about these, John," I said. He replied, "Oh, those. I

bought them in the airport in Nairobi and had my painter do them up. Souvenirs, you know."

In late 1975 I had answered an interviewer's question: Whose house would I like to show that hadn't been featured anywhere? Without pause, I blurted out,

ABOVE: The living room of Gore Vidal's Hollywood Hills home. The novelist hired longtime friend Diana Phipps to do the interiors. RIGHT: Vidal bought the 1929 Spanish Colonial Revival house in 1977 and owned it until his passing in 2012. September 1980

ABOVE: President and Mrs. Reagan's bedroom at the White House. RIGHT: The West Sitting Hall, which the couple used as a living room, included furnishings brought from their home in Los Angeles by Ted Graber. December 1981

The First Lady's office was primarily furnished with pieces from the White House collection. Items were pulled from storage and refinished as part of the months-long renovation. New additions included the 18th-century daybed.

127

"Truman Capote!" Several days later I realized I had better contact Mr. Capote ASAP and try to persuade him to let us photograph his house in the Hamptons. To my relief, he agreed. Did I put Mr. Capote on the cover or at least do a cover blurb naming him as the visited? No. Well, in defense of my denseness, the magazine was distributed only by "better newsstands and bookstores," which meant I only gave a passing thought to the cover as a sales tool. No cover blurbs. No celebrity on the cover. That would change when the reality and benefits of newsstand sales were pointed out!

A few years later, at a party held at the Beverly Hills restaurant The Bistro, a waiter came up to me and whispered that Mr. Capote would like to meet me. Deep breathe to quell my fear. He was one of the great writers of our time, and I had read everything he had written. Capote was seated on a banquette and asked me to be seated. After pleasantries, he said in that legendary falsetto, "Maybe you can help me with a problem." I just nodded my head, unable to speak. "It's about my house in the Hamptons. The one you photographed." Oh-oh. He's going to complain about something. "In the back entry, the floorboards are warped. What can I do about that?" At a complete

When Baron Guy de Rothschild gave his Château de Ferrières to the Universities of Paris in 1977, he asked architect Augustin Julia to build a chalet on the property for him and his wife, Marie-Hélène. The living room included a Lalanne sheep and exotic sculptures and textiles. April 1987

The baroness's bedroom at Ferrières was
upholstered in an antique Indonesian fabric and
furnished with a daybed, a Brazilian nightstand
and a Louis XV *bureau plat*. The 18th-century
Chinese painting is of French missionaries.

LEFT: John Dickinson designed the San Francisco home of the city's Chief of Protocol Charlotte Mailliard Shultz, then Charlotte Mailliard Swig. ABOVE: The dining room included a *trompe-l'oeil* rug and a portrait of Napoléon Bonaparte's nephews, relatives of the Mailliard family. May 1989

ARCHITECTURAL DIGEST

THE INTERNATIONAL MAGAZINE OF FINE INTERIOR DESIGN

OCTOBER 1989 $4.50

The foldout cover of the October 1989 issue featured the mirrored salon of Jean-François Daigre's Louis XVI home in Paris, which he created with his design partner, Valerian Rybar. The Hall of Mirrors at Versailles served as the opulent room's inspiration.

loss, I could only reply, "I have no idea." At that blessed moment, dinner was announced.

In the story, which ran in the January-February issue of 1976, Truman explained that his Hamptons house was his "place to be alone." Of the interiors, which he did himself, he said, "For me, it's a bore to use a decorator. I know exactly what I want. I just don't care to have someone come in and tell me what I need to live with. I know.'"

There was a house I wasn't sure I could get for the magazine: Fred Astaire's. How it began, I do not recall, but there I was with an assistant ringing his doorbell. He answered the door himself, welcomed us and showed us around the house, stopping in the hall at a photograph. "Isn't she beautiful?" It was his late wife. We went into the living room, which was dominated by a pool table. "Mr. Astaire," I said, "could we photograph you in your home?" "I think so," he replied, warily. As we were leaving, he said, "Wait," and sat at a small piano nearby. He played for a couple of minutes, then asked what we thought of his new composition. "Charming." "Wonderful." "I'm really still not sure I want to be pho-tographed in my house. It's very personal, as you can see." Oh, no. He was backing out. "Mr. Astaire, I prom-ise that the writer who interviews you will not ask you who your favorite dancing partner was." He laughed. "Well, then I guess it's all right."

Michael Taylor's house on a cliff in San Francisco was somehow opulent with surprising simplicity. I put the living room on the cover. Space, line, proportion were his essentials. "Nothing is a prop and nothing is here simply for effect," he said. Maybe. His bedroom housed what is arguably the most dramatic bed ever. Seventeenth-century Spanish. Carved wood. Gold leaf. Neither photographs nor layouts could capture Mi-chael's extraordinary talent. He often called me on Sun-day afternoons to discuss projects. He was one of the greats, if not the all-time greatest interior designer.

The designers placed a Régence mirror above a Louis XV marble fireplace at the far end of the room. In the foreground, a pair of leather-upholstered Louis XV chairs joined a trio of poufs covered in a gray satin hand-painted to resemble stone.

136

ABOVE: Along with their chalet at Ferrières, the
Rothschilds owned Château de Meautry in Normandy,
which the baroness decorated with François Catroux.
RIGHT: The living room featured 16th- and 17th-
century furnishings and artworks, including a landscape
by Pieter Brueghel the Younger. September 1990

In the dining room at Meautry, the baroness displayed a collection of faience commissioned by her grandfather. Beyond the dining room was the library, where she placed a 16th-century celestial globe on the writing table.

ARCHITECTURAL DIGEST

THE INTERNATIONAL MAGAZINE OF FINE INTERIOR DESIGN

JULY 1982 $4.00

CHAPTER FOUR

1982-1992

This Is Work?

The San Francisco home of art dealer John Berggruen, designed
by Andrew K. Belschner and Beverly Thome. July 1982

T he success of the White House issue set the tone for the rest of the decade, a period of continued growth reflecting an era that became synonymous with extravagance and wealth. Traditional interiors dominated the pages, which included visits to Queen Beatrix of the Netherlands, Rudolf Nureyev in Paris and Yves Saint Laurent in Marrakesh—but there were exciting surprises too, like a Mongolian yurt. In keeping with a boom in collecting, AD published its first "Art and Antiques" annual in 1984 as a special thirteenth issue. The following year welcomed a host of literary contributors, including Truman Capote, William Styron, Kurt Vonnegut, Gerald Clarke, John Updike, Susan Sheehan and Judith Thurman.

ABOVE: Queen Beatrix and Prince Claus of the Netherlands. RIGHT: The queen restored Huis ten Bosch, a 17th-century summer palace, as her official residence in The Hague. May 1982

ABOVE: Grey Gardens, in East Hampton, New York.
RIGHT: Sally Quinn and Ben Bradlee renovated the
1897 home with architect E. L. Futterman. Quinn restored
furnishings she found in the attic, like the chaises
and wicker chairs in the living room. December 1984

Architects wrote too, like Robert A.M. Stern and Michael Graves, as did W columnist Aileen Mehle, known as Suzy. Even His Royal Highness the Prince of Wales penned a guest speaker column.

Architectural Digest of the 1980s and early 1990s defined glamour. It was the place designers chose to share their own homes, among them Kalef Alaton, Axel Vervoordt, Peter Marino, Benjamin Baldwin, Angelo Donghia, Marjorie Reed, Geoffrey Bradfield, Thomas Britt, Valerian Rybar, Albert Hadley, Robert Bray, Juan Pablo Molyneux and Karin Blake. Celebrities of all fields were featured, too: fashion designers Carolina Herrera and Geoffrey Beene; artists Andrew Wyeth, Jeremiah Goodman and Claude and François-Xavier Lalanne; Hollywood figures Robert Altman, David Geffen, Norman Lear, Steven Spielberg and Mike Nichols; actors Candice Bergen, Mary Tyler Moore, Joan Crawford, John Wayne and Marlon Brando; performers David Bowie, Luciano Pavarotti, Madonna and Zubin Mehta; and writers as diverse as Gore Vidal and Dr. Seuss.

The first of many themed issues, "The English Country House," appeared in June 1985. The following spring "Architectural Digest Travels" was published as a supplement with

Domed yurts on the steppe of Inner Mongolia brought indigenous architecture to readers' attention. Designed to be collapsible, they could be transported by their nomadic inhabitants as they traveled the grasslands with their herds. The yurts were constructed of wood and wool felt and traditionally featured a red door. July 1982

The entrance hall of the Manhattan home of Juan-Pablo Molyneux and his wife, Pilar, shared not only a 16th-century relief by Giambologna and 19th-century bronze Egyptian figures but also custom Harley-Davidson and BMW motorcycles. September 1999

the hope of a creating a spin-off title, and in 1987 the magazine debuted its first "Before & After" issue.

The early 1990s marked another pivotal point in the magazine's history. In 1990 AD sponsored a series of panel discussions at the Smithsonian Institution and published its first AD100 issue, which profiled the magazine's top architects and designers of the year and set a new industry standard. It also published its first Academy Awards issue and made its "Discoveries by Designers" column a monthly feature (the popular shopping section first appeared as a supplement in 1988). Other themed issues included "Designers' Own Homes," "American Country Houses," and "Exotic Homes." To mark Rense's twentieth year at the magazine, Bud Knapp took out an entire page in The New York Times *on October 22, 1990. It featured her portrait and the title, "This Page is for Paige." In it, he celebrated her reaching a readership of more than three million, adding, "The greatest editors are few and far between. Paige Rense is one of them."*

A few years later, the magazine was again making headlines but not for design news. In November of 1992 Knapp decided to sell—and not just Architectural Digest *but also its sister publication,* Bon Appétit. *Two extremely successful titles were on the market, with some thirty suitors offering bids. It was international news and one of the most closely watched deals in publishing history.*

MY FRIEND FROM THE BEGINNING

For forty-some years Mario Buatta has designed extraordinary interiors combining fine design with shelter, comfort and joy. He is a legend. His color palette cheers, delights and offers emotional sustenance. It seems impossible to imagine being depressed in one of his rooms. Personally, he also cheers and delights. He is a practical joker (look out for gold-plated creepy-crawlies), and he genuinely cares about his clients, who quickly become loyalists who appreciate his work and his friendship.

It was always a pleasure to show his work, in part because of the fan mail we received from our readers (a Mario Buatta interior on the cover meant big newsstand sales), but he was also very important to the magazine's early success. When I became editor, I

went to New York City to meet with major designers, hoping to persuade them to give me their work first. (It was an unwritten law in the field that if a designer showed their work in one magazine, no other magazine would touch it.) Mario was one of the first major designers to believe what I said about *Architectural Digest*'s future, and he introduced me to everyone. It has been over four decades since he came into my professional and personal life. He took me to see Bobby Short perform in the Carlyle Hotel shortly after we met. I remember thinking, "This is work?"

On one of those early trips to New York City, Mario Buatta took me to a client's housewarming party, and it was there, all those years ago, that I first met Marjorie Reed Gordon. She welcomed me to New York and invited me to dinner—and she wasn't even a professional decorator. I have known and admired her for at least three decades and observed with great interest her growth as an interior designer. When I first saw the townhouse interior she designed for herself, I wished I could move right in. She continues to design wonderful homes for clients, and always with *them* in mind. There is no "Marjorie Reed look." She understands that her work is for her client, not for publicity, and she only works with people she likes. I would hire her anytime.

MY FIRST FEW CALLS

Who were the first interior designers I interviewed after joining *Architectural Digest*? Well, first was Michael Greer, on the phone from New York. What was my first question? Not in my memory bank, but I will never forget his answer: "That question is so tiresome." The following year, after we showed his apartment in the January-February 1974 issue, he gave a cocktail party for me. The movie star Joan Bennett was among the brave first arrivals. (I always think first arrivals are brave.) She sat on a sofa with me. As new guests came over, I rose to greet them. Joan said, "Sit down. You don't have to jump up." I sat. Just two

The September 1985 cover featured Rudolf Nureyev in the drawing room of his home in Paris. Art director Emilio Carcano designed the lavish, theatrical interiors.

ARCHITECTURAL DIGEST

THE INTERNATIONAL MAGAZINE OF FINE INTERIOR DESIGN

SEPTEMBER 1985 $4.50

ABOVE: A marble study of Pauline Bonaparte, Princess Borghese, by Antonio Canova, and a portrait of William Linley, attributed to Sir Thomas Lawrence, in the living room of Gore Vidal's Roman penthouse. RIGHT: Luciano Moroni filled the interiors with an eclectic mix of 18th- and 19th-century art and antiques. The moldings were *faux marbre*. October 1985

Bear House, one of several storybook structures at Wyntoon, the Northern California retreat of William Randolph Hearst, built by Julia Morgan in the 1930s. January 1988. FOLLOWING PAGES: The covers of the first issues of the "AD100," August 1990, and the "AD100 Architects," August 1991.

ARCHITECTURAL DIGEST
THE AD 100

AUGUST 15, 1990

AN EXCLUSIVE GUIDE TO THE WORLD'S

FINEST INTERIOR DESIGNERS

PLUS SHOWROOMS, ANTIQUES

SHOPS AND ART GALLERIES

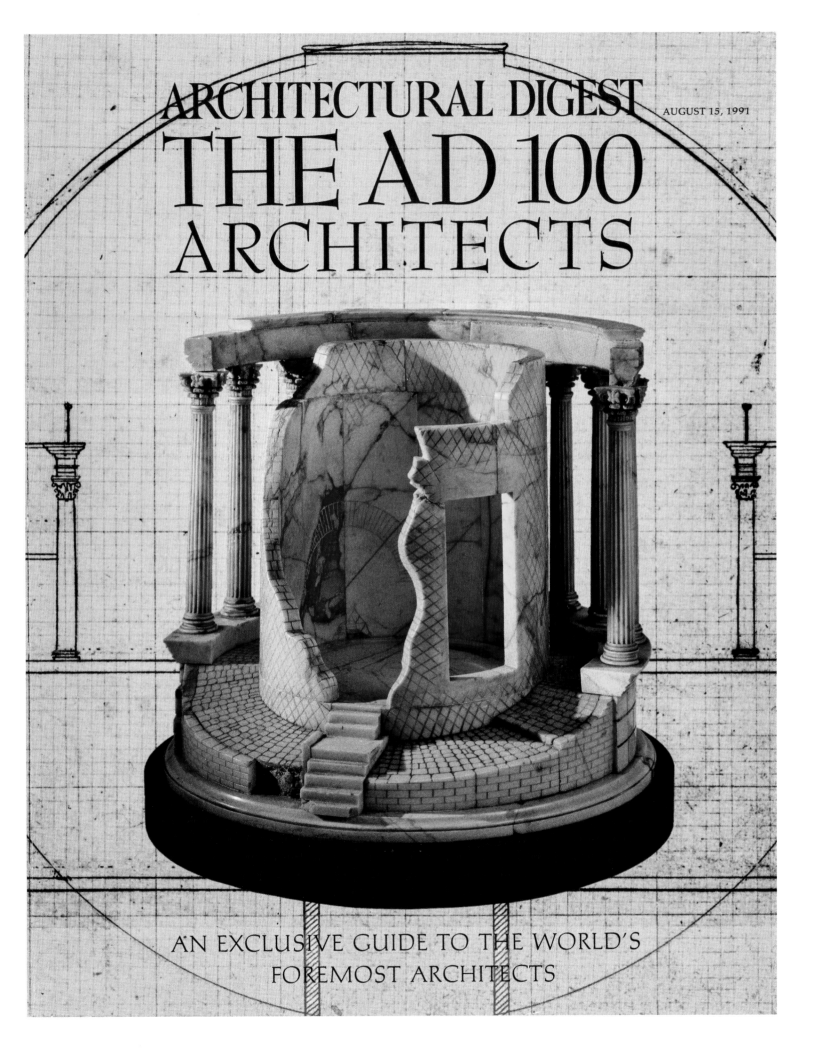

THE AD 100
ARCHITECTS

AN EXCLUSIVE GUIDE TO THE WORLD'S
FOREMOST ARCHITECTS

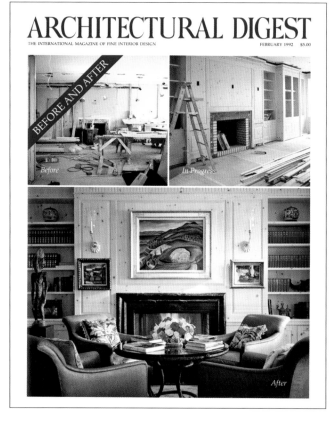

years later, Michael was murdered in that very apartment by an unfortunate choice of acquaintances.

My second designer interview was Sally Sirkin Lewis. She had just opened a showroom in West Los Angeles (J. Robert Scott, named for her son) and filled it with sophisticated, understated furniture by the leading designers of that time, as well as her own designs. People told her the showroom would fail. They told her Los Angeles was "not ready" for such a sophisticated "New York look." Sally thought that was nonsense. She held fast to her faith in the work she presented. She was right. Word spread. Interior designers on the West Coast were impressed. Soon designers from New York and throughout the country embraced her work.

ABOVE: The "Before & After" and "American Country Houses" issues were favorites of *AD* readers. Seen here are the February 1992 and June 1989 covers.
RIGHT: The "Academy Awards" issue debuted in April 1990 and revisited Grauman's Chinese Theatre, where Paige Rense once worked as an usherette.

Sally's interiors for clients were featured in *AD* many times. She became known internationally and opened showrooms in London, Chicago and Manhattan. She established a factory in Los Angeles for her own custom work and designed fabrics in Europe to be sold in her showrooms. Sally believed in herself. Believed in her vision. Believed those who said she couldn't do it were wrong, and she was right.

IN MEMORIAM

A memorial service for Truman Capote was held at the celebrity cemetery in Westwood, California. His friend Joanna Carson—at whose house he had been a frequent guest and indeed died there—was in charge of the sad event. She greeted everyone with clipboard in hand and assigned seats. I was seated behind Jack Lemmon and his wife, Felicia Farr, and Walter Matthau and his wife, Carol, with her renowned white make-up. Christopher Isherwood spoke briefly, along with a few others. Artie Shaw was the most memorable because he began by saying, "I don't know why I'm here. I didn't know Tru-

ARCHITECTURAL DIGEST

THE INTERNATIONAL MAGAZINE OF FINE INTERIOR DESIGN

APRIL 1990 $5.00

man Capote." At the end of the service, we left blinking in the bright sunshine after being in the semi-darkness of the chapel. Several mourners spoke of touring the cemetery to see where stars were buried or entombed. Well, Westwood is next to Hollywood, with its tours to stars' homes, so it was a natural transition.

OUR FIRST SPECIAL ISSUE

In June 1985 *AD* published its first themed issue, "The English Country House," which we did in conjunction with the exhibition *The Treasure Houses of Britain*, at the National Gallery in Washington, D.C. In the issue, David Mlinaric told us the secrets of English style: "There was once a client for whom we made some really beautiful curtains. When I went back to the house about six weeks later, I found she had actually slashed the edges of the three pair in the drawing room. She had shredded the cloth because she found them too good, too new. All in all, the keynote of English style is informality." Also in the issue was an article titled "Beautiful Breeds: Portraits of Man's Best Friend." As a dedicated supporter of the Humane Society of the United States, I have a special interest in dogs that are rescued from puppy mills, organized dog fighting and other cruelties. These portraits of canine nobility are treasures for those who share my feelings.

But it's really all creatures that I love, and I'm a vegetarian now. Ken once took me to the Huka Lodge in New Zealand ("A home away from home," Queen Elizabeth II once called it), hoping I might develop an interest in fishing. I did like standing in a beautiful stream in high rubber boots but I confessed to the guide that didn't want to catch a fish and see it struggling for its life. He told me, "Don't worry, it will probably be Old Ed. He's been caught so many times, he knows we'll release him." I didn't become a fishing enthusiast, but I did like the Huka Lodge very much. If you go and catch Old Ed, be sure to give him my regards as you release him.

The dining room of Evelyn and Leonard Lauder's Manhattan home, designed by Marjorie Reed Gordon. The room doubled as a library and was hung with the Lauders' collection of early-20th-century travel posters. December 2009

I first met Malcolm Forbes when he invited me to lunch in his building. We chatted about magazines, and he later invited me to many events, which I was always delighted to attend. He invited me to join his staff and family at a balloon meet at his château in France and to his *palais* in Morocco, which he hoped I would publish. I told him I couldn't—it just wasn't good enough, and he laughed. In fact, he seemed to enjoy telling everyone that I had turned him down. He never held it against me and later invited me to his homes in London, New Jersey and Colorado. I visited eight of his homes. Once, as a thank-you, I gave a dinner for him at the Carlyle Hotel. He asked if he could bring a guest. It turned out to be Elizabeth Taylor. She made a late entrance, and the restaurant fell silent as she glided to the table, where she took her seat next to

ABOVE: David Bowie at the doors to the dining pavilion of the Mustique home he shared with his wife, Iman. RIGHT: Bowie worked with architect Arne Hasselqvist and designer Linda Garland on the Indonesian-style property. September 1992

Malcolm. During dinner, she turned to me and asked, "Paige, don't you think Malcolm has the look of a man who wants to buy me jewelry?" We three knew my response would be "Yes." All the guests commented on her beauty, and her knowledge of AIDS.

A few years later I was a guest on Malcolm's yacht, *Highlander*, sailing from Hawaii to the Fiji island he owned. On the island, he showed me the site he had selected for his burial place. At that time, it seemed that the site would never be occupied because Malcolm would clearly be immortal. I was wrong. He was a charismatic host of unique charm. I am only one of many who miss him.

ON SCOUTING HOMES

This is what usually happened: An interior decorator or architect would contact me, or a member of my staff, to arrange for me to see a house or an apartment. If I had reason to believe I would want to show the work to our readers, I would see it personally. If the work was by someone unknown to us, I would ask for photographs to be sent to me, stressing that they need not be by a professional photographer. Next, an appointment would be

The living room of Madonna's New York City apartment, designed by her brother Christopher Ciccone, featured Art Déco furnishings by Eugène Printz and Dominique, among others. Above the fireplace was an oil by Léger; to the right was a painting by Dalí. November 1991

166

ARCHITECTURAL DIGEST

SPRING 1987

TRAVELS

Architect's Villas on Anguilla

Inside the Salzburg Festival

Collectors' Finds in Spain

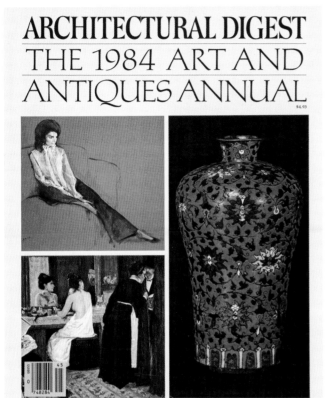

made. I always asked that, if possible, the client-resident not be present in order to avoid lots of conversation and my having to say no to the client in front of the designer, if asked. Without hindrance, I walked through at a good pace, thanked whomever for letting me see the interior, and left—the key was to never sit down. If the news was good, I would tell the designer that our photographer liaison, James Huntington, would be in touch to work out a time for our shoot and give the name of the photographer who would be coming. Yes or no. That was that. When I was on the road, the first houses I would see were generally by established designers, but then, like circles in pond, I would work outward. By the fourth visit, I knew I was getting somewhere I wanted to be.

LEFT: The cover of the Spring 1987 "Travels" issue featured an Anguilla project, Covecastles, by architect Myron Goldfinger. ABOVE, LEFT AND RIGHT: Special issues included the 1984 "Art and Antiques" annual and the September 1987 "Architecture," which showed a tile fountain created for a Moore Ruble Yudell–designed house in Beverly Hills.

Secure designers would tell me about others that were not yet so well known.

Years ago I was in Honolulu scouting for interiors. A very nice newspaper columnist, whom I had met not long before in Los Angeles, gave a cocktail party for me. She also invited Clare Boothe Luce, who was living in Hawaii at that time. She opened the introduction saying, "One great editor should meet another great editor." Mrs. Luce turned her back and walked away. At first it seemed just rude, but, thinking about it later, being an editor was the least of her career. After all, she had been a Republican member for the House of Representatives, a playwright and the U.S. ambassador to Italy. A few years later at an event in New York City, another editor asked Bill Blass to be "presented" to me. He made the introduction; she nodded briefly and turned away. Clearly, I was not an editor other editors cared to know.

ON SAYING NO

Nothing ever got in the magazine because it was expensive. I turned down multi-million-dollar homes all

ARCHITECTURAL DIGEST

THE INTERNATIONAL MAGAZINE OF FINE INTERIOR DESIGN

JULY 1986 $4.50

ART FEATURE:
BEAUTIFUL BREEDS

the time. The most common phone call I used to get was someone saying, "You will love this home; it cost millions!" I really resented that. Of course the homes we showed were costly—we didn't have an abiding interest in showing how to make umbrella stands out of pegboard—but it was not about money. Money and taste do not have a relationship. If people think a price tag is a criterion, they are dead wrong. What I needed was a polite way to say no, which, along with *rejection*, sounded too harsh. I had been offered bribes to publish homes, and sometimes when I turned people down, they threatened me. We eventually decided that the nicest way to let people down was something

OPPOSITE: Thomas Earl's *West Highland White Terrier*, circa 1870, greeted readers of the July 1986 issue. ABOVE: In the early 1890s Austrian painter Carl Kahler was commissioned by an American millionaire to paint her forty-two angora cats, titled by her husband *My Wife's Lovers*.

we called "Not for *AD*," or "NFAD" internally. I composed a form letter, explaining that the magazine could not publish the work because "it just wasn't right for *AD* at this time." Rooms are like people—some beautiful, some not. For *AD*, they had to be photogenic. I've rejected lovely homes that somehow lacked that elusive quality that would have made them good for the magazine. I was always after a certain magic. It was hard to define. I knew it when I saw it.

But sometimes I was told no, too. I would have photographed Katharine Hepburn's house if it had two army cots and a lamp. She said no, but I kept working on her. Years later, a friend who worked with Kate told me over dinner that she sometimes prowled around neighborhood houses at night, peeking into windows. What a story! I wrote to her what I hoped was a lighthearted note asking if she could write a short piece about her Peeping Tom adventures. Her handwritten reply: "I just can't."

In March 1988 we featured an "Artist's Dia-

logue" with Kenneth Noland by curator and critic Karen Wilkin. (At the time this interview took place, I knew Ken only as an admired acquaintance—we were not married until 1994.) A phrase of Ken's close friend, sculptor David Smith, comes to mind. He had spoken of combining painting and sculpture into a new art form that would "beat either one." Though Ken always presented his paintings in coherent series, he explored a wide range of images: circles, chevrons, diamonds, stripes, plaids and an extraordinary group of shaped canvases. And many "oddball pictures" too, some abandoned, some stored mentally for future use. "I have to work things out by painting them," he said. "I have to do it and see it. That's the only way I find out if it will go anywhere."

Looking back through the issues, there are so many wonderful glimpses into the minds of some of the world's greatest architects and designers, like Renzo Mongiardino, whose feats of *trompe l'oeil* became his trademark. "Renzo," a Venetian friend once said, "approaches beauty with the modesty and rigor of a monk and the nonchalance of a lord." Perhaps the most memorable quote he gave us during one of our many interviews was, "You must take what you need from the past, but you must mock it when necessary, and you must make it yours."

In the very, very early days of *AD*, architect Philip

Johnson spurned us with these words: "*Architectural Digest* is pornography for architects." He later recanted and became a fan.

I first met Juan Pablo Molyneaux years ago, when he was part of a design show house. His part of the show was very good and quite original. I asked him to show me his interior design work in the future. He did and I was happy to publish it. He said, "When a place is right, it works a kind of spell, a magic you're aware of immediately." True. I once asked J.P., as friends know him, what style he works in and his answer was immediate: "Continental." He is the son of an English father and a Chilean mother, raised in Europe and Latin America, and educated in architecture both in Santiago and at the Ecole des Beaux-Arts and the Ecole du Louvre in Paris. "Continental" was not a surprising answer. He lives with his beautiful wife, Pilar, in a Manhattan townhouse, where he also worked. Through the years we have become friends, sharing not only an interest in design but strong, protective beliefs about animal welfare. Today he divides his time between New York and France, when he is not on airplanes designing en route for oligarchs and moguls.

In May 1988 we showed the Los Angeles apartment of designer Kalef Alaton, who remarked, "I love the bare and the cluttered." He had purchased an apartment building in West Hollywood notable more for its

LEFT: The entrance to Blair-Lee House, one of the four residences that make up Blair House, the presidential guest house in Washington, D.C. RIGHT: The cover of the October 1988 issue celebrated the property's restoration done under the direction of Chief of Protocol Selwa Roosevelt, seen at right with Mark Hampton, seated, and Mario Buatta, who collaborated on the redesign.

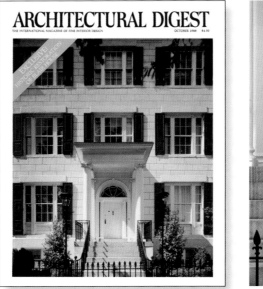

The entrance hall to Blair House was designed by Hampton, who incorporated such pieces as the Philadelphia Empire pier table and the circa 1792 English tallcase clock. The Blair House Restoration Fund was established in 1985 to maintain the historic property.

celebrity associations—Marilyn Monroe, Frank Sinatra—than for its architecture. Turkish himself, he hired a young Turkish architect to remodel the interior. They installed a spiral stair to wind upward through it. With no handrails, I might add. (Once, I and several other party guests had to sit and bump down stair by stair, so daunting was it.) Alaton said he bought art "on impulse—for love," and that the important thing was how you lived with it. "If you want to put it on a pedestal or in a spotlight, with nothing in front of it, then you should live in a museum." He derided those who collected only with an eye to status or resale value, declaring he was "tired of looking at paintings with price tags."

LEFT: Sally Sirkin Lewis opened her showroom, J. Robert Scott, in the early 1970s. The May 1987 issue profiled the designer and her latest pieces in its "Design Dialogue" column. ABOVE: Vignettes highlighted her interest in reinterpreting classic furniture forms in contemporary proportions.

THE "ACADEMY AWARDS" ISSUE

In April 1990 we published our special "Academy Awards" issue, the first of eight such collectors' editions that came to be known as the "Hollywood at Home" issues. (They ultimately led to our 2005 book of the same title.) The issue featured many stars, directors and producers: King Vidor, Mary Pickford and Douglas Fairbanks, Ernst Lubitsch, William Powell, David O. Selznick, Harold Lloyd, Gloria Swanson, Irene Dunne, Warner Baxter (once described as "Valentino without a horse"), Gary Cooper, Edward G. Robinson (with his highly regarded art collection), James Cagney, Hal Roach, Spencer Tracy, Katharine Hepburn, Myrna Loy, Marlene Dietrich, Victor Fleming, Merle Oberon, Melvyn Douglas, Barbara Stanwyck and Robert Taylor, Norma Shearer and Irving Thalberg, Fredric March, Claudette Colbert, George Cukor, Marlon Brando, Alfred Hitchcock, Lillian Gish, John Wayne, Fred Astaire, Liza Minnelli, Bette

ABOVE: Chatsworth House, the family seat of the dukes of Devonshire, is surrounded by gardens designed by "Capability" Brown and Joseph Paxton. RIGHT: The house, then home to Deborah and Andrew Cavendish, the eleventh duke and duchess of Devonshire, is one of England's most important estates and was featured in the magazine several times over the years. October 1988

ABOVE: Malcolm Forbes with one of two Harley-Davidsons he kept on board his yacht, *Highlander*. RIGHT: The yacht, designed by Jon Bannenberg, sailing in New York Harbor against the backdrop of the Twin Towers. January 1987

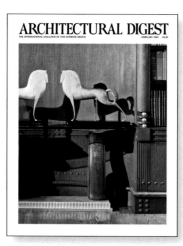

ABOVE: Malcolm Forbes purchased the Fijian
island of Laucala in 1972. The main house
was built in the early 1900s in the British
Colonial style. RIGHT: The island was a retreat
for family and friends, as well as a working
coconut plantation. February 1989

informality remains the keynote, and while dogs flop thankfully down on the kitchen's cool flagstones, Chloe is given unlimited space in which to position her toys.

Up one flight of the imposing stone staircase, the living room suggests quite a different style of life. Books, pictures and furniture blend into a natural whole, as if everything had been acquired over generations.

Antique shawls and strongly patterned rugs lend a warmth to this main salon—a quality the Malles particularly appreciate when they manage to spend a few days in Lot in winter. Warmth of another kind is communicated by a large colorful painting that beams an evocation of native life in India across the room.

"I don't know how Indian it really is," says Louis Malle with a grin. "I

think it might have been inspired by a postcard. But for years it hung in a café in Arles, and it amused me. When the café was modernized, I bought it. We felt the salon would be the best place to hang it, and what's strange is that now it looks as if it had been there forever. That's what is fascinating about this house; time does stand still. In that sense, the place is literally enchanted."□

OPPOSITE: On the kitchen wall at right is a 19th-century salon painting of Hecate and her dogs. "The *real* dog is a Pyrenees sheepdog named Nourson," says Candice Bergen. "He is on his lunch break, which lasts all day." ABOVE: A large stone mantel in the master bedroom is original to the house. The 17th-century country pine bench-table rests between a pair of 19th-century armchairs. BELOW: The 15th-century round tower, the oldest part of the house, was a fortification that overlooked the valley.

"I shot both *Lacombe Lucien* and *Black Moon* in the area and used the barn as an editing room."

118

Davis, Gene Hackman, Kirk Douglas, Clark Gable and Carole Lombard, Bogart and Bacall, Joan Crawford and more. It was a huge success.

TELEVISION APPEARANCES

Suddenly, TV was the thing and afternoon talk shows started asking me to appear and talk about celebrity houses published by the magazine. The first, I think, was Dinah Shore's show. She was gracious and charming. I showed slides of celebrity houses. Did it maybe three or four times, then I screwed up. Talking about window treatments (drapes, curtains, etc.), I said, "Windows can be a pane." The audience groaned. I was never asked back. Later, Phil Donahue asked me to guest... with, of course, celebrity slides. I walked onto the set and almost ran away—Joan Rivers was Phil's guest co-host. My thought was, "I'm toast." Although funny, she could be acerbic and cutting. I thought, "I'm

about to be her victim." No. It didn't happen. I don't remember her saying much, if anything. I had escaped. Phil asked me on several more times, and it was always a pleasure. That was the totality of my television career. Cut. No one ever asked me again. Until Charlie Rose, twice in the late 1990s, and CBS *Sunday Morning* in 2003.

A PRINCE CHARLES WEEKEND

After meeting Joan Rivers on the set of Phil Donahue's show I did not encounter her again until some years later, on a plane to London with Ken. Turned out

ABOVE: Pages from the June 1988 issue showed the summer haven of Louis Malle and Candice Bergen and their daughter, Chloe. Malle restored the house, set in France's Lot Valley, in the late 1960s. RIGHT: Bergen and Malle in front of the house, part of which dates to the 15th century. June 1988

we were both going to the Prince's Trust weekend, hosted by Prince Charles. The first event was a formal dinner at Buckingham Palace. Upon entering, we were greeted by the prince and his aide, who told him quietly the name and "credit" for each person on presentation. Later, during cocktails, Camilla introduced herself and said *Architectural Digest* was her favorite magazine. The royals always knew just what to say. (Our "royal," Elizabeth Taylor, once told me the same thing.) Ken thought Camilla was quite sexy. "I didn't think she would be so pretty," he told me. The next day we went to the Ascot races, and that evening there was a large, tented dinner at the prince's country house, emceed by Joan, who sat next to the prince. Joan was thoughtful and well read, quite the opposite of her public persona. I subsequently published several of her houses. Her Beverly Hills home was designed for entertaining—hostessed by the *real* Joan Rivers.

Estée Lauder invited me for lunch one day, and before our food was served, I learned that she felt we had a bond because I had remarried my husband Arthur Rense and she had remarried her husband, Joseph Lauder. I remember from our conversation, "You should wear raspberry lipstick." I searched a long time for that shade.

Lyn and Norman Lear found their Los Angeles house just shortly after they wed in 1987. The couple renovated the house to include a two-story library, screening room and space for their collections of antiques and contemporary art. July 1992

LEFT, ABOVE AND BELOW:
Couturier Valentino purchased
a villa near the Appian Way in
Rome in 1972 and decorated it
with Renzo Mongiardino.
They imbued the home with
Asian accents like Chinese
stenciled walls in the entrance
hall and blue-and-white
ceramics in the dining room.
RIGHT: Floral prints, a French
needlepoint carpet and an
embroidered-velvet bench
filled the living room.
Chinese figures made for the
Royal Pavilion at Brighton
stood on an Italian rococo
table. September 1988.
FOLLOWING PAGES: Philip
Johnson's 1949 Glass House, a
gemlike box of glass, steel and
brick, was the first structure
and the main living space
on the architect's New Canaan,
Connecticut, compound.
November 1986

I had been spending a lot of time in Washington, D.C., doing a design program as a fundraiser. Each program featured different designers and architects over a six-week period. During one period, I received an invitation from Hillary Clinton to lunch at her home. Two fellows who lived next door to her had helped her move into her house and they asked her to give a "ladies lunch" for me. Several women on her staff were there, along with the grande dame of the Democratic Party, Susan Mary Alsop. Hillary was funny, self-deprecating and humble. She was just one of the girls. As we finished our lunch, Bill Clinton came onto the patio and was introduced to each woman around the tale. He stopped behind me and massaged my shoulders. Could life hold anything more?

I cannot recall how I met Geoffrey Beene, but we were having lunch in New York City one day, and he said he would like it if I wore clothing from his line exclusively. Stunned, I protested, "But I'm too short to do justice to your designs." He said, "That doesn't matter; one of my biggest markets is Japan!"

Jimmy Stewart kissed me. I gave a large dinner for Richard Meier, who was designing the Getty, at David Murdock's Regency Club that included Gloria

Kalef Alaton hired Turkish architect Haluk Yorgancioglu to turn a five-unit, 1950s apartment building in West Hollywood into a single home and guesthouse. He centered the living room on a 19th-century Baccarat chandler, adding a pair of Louis XV fauteuils signed *Gourdin*, an antique Chinese table and a Régence mirror. May 1988

and Jimmy Stewart. A few days before, I had called Gloria, asking if *Architectural Digest* could photograph their home, which I had heard was charming. She said, "Oh, no. I would have to have the upholstery cleaned and send out the slipcovers." We laughed, and I invited her and, of course, her husband to the upcoming dinner. She accepted. As they were leaving the dinner, Jimmy gave me a courtesy thank-you and a goodnight kiss, on both cheeks. Well, I do exaggerate at times.

I first met Joan Fontaine at a fundraising party for the historic Swan House in Atlanta. We hit it off and hung out together, planning to get together in New York on our return. And we did. She gave me lunch in her Manhattan apartment, then gave me the tour. The last room she showed me was her bedroom. "Oh, if that bed could talk. You see the bedside table? Well, I used to put a glass of ice water there, and if a man was getting too excited too soon, I just grabbed his hand and put it in the water. It always worked." A few weeks later, I accepted her invitation to visit her for a weekend in her Carmel, California, house. (She loved the climate, because she could play golf year-round.) The second evening we went to the home of gay friends of hers for drinks. The next day she told me, "You know, they think we are lesbians." "Why?" I asked. "Dear girl, because we are spending the weekend together." Oh. Remember when two men or two women would share an apartment or house they could only afford as a share? All different now. Wow.

One day a friend asked if I wanted to talk to Jacqueline Kennedy Onassis about book possibilities. She was an editor at the time with Doubleday. Obviously, I said yes. We met in the dining room of the Carlyle Hotel. She said, "My arm is longer on this side," and sat down, putting a heavy bag of books on the floor. We chatted briefly about our mutual friends, and then she asked me if I would be inter-

Alaton's bedroom featured twin canopied beds and a Regency center table. The room doubled as a library for his collection of art and design books. The home exemplified the designer's talent for integrating classic furnishings with contemporary architecture.

ABOVE: The "Hollywood at Home" issues featured stars throughout movie history in their private residences, such as James Stewart in Beverly Hills (April 1990) and Helen Mirren in New Orleans (April 1998). RIGHT: Spencer Tracy at his Encino, California, ranch. April 1990

ested in working with Doubleday on several *Architectural Digest* books on interiors. "We would work together," she said. My answer was yes. She told me she would talk to Doubleday about it and let me know. A few weeks went by. No word. I called our mutual friend and asked if he had heard anything. "No, but I'll call her." He did. Soon her soft voice was on my home phone: "I'm sorry I haven't called sooner. Could you come to a meeting at the Doubleday offices to discuss?" "Yes." We set a date and time. As I recall, we were six at a table for the meeting: Jackie, me and four men in suits. As we began talking about interior design books, Jackie teased one of them who had mentioned a bit of decorating terminology with: "You know about *chinoiserie!*" We all agreed that the *Architectural Digest* books were a good project for all, and the meeting ended. We published *Decorating for Celebrities* in 1980 but never worked with them again.

We published later books with Abrams.

We never published Jackie's own homes but she did feature in the issues from time to time. In September 1996, writer Susan Mary Alsop, a friend of the former First Lady's, shared a remembrance I particularly enjoyed. "While in the White House, Jackie formed a small committee to assist her in redecorating the White House soon after the inauguration and I was one of the members," wrote Susan. "Our chairman was Henry E. du Pont, the great collector and expert on Americana. One day when we were expecting his visit, we met in the Red Room and we were admiring a small still life oil painting we had hung when Mr. du Pont arrived. He took one look at the picture and said, 'Ladies, surely you are aware that still lifes are only for dining rooms.' We stood abashed until Jackie, as usual, saved the day. 'Oh, Mr. du Pont, it just shows how little we know. Goodness, we are lucky to have you to teach us what to do. That still life will come down immediately.' It did, that very morning. Months later, my husband, Joseph, and I were in the Red Room. I saw to my astonishment that the picture was back. By chance, Mr. du Pont came in as I was regarding it. I asked him how he thought the new arrangement looked. He answered, 'Everything looks splendid. Jackie really does have a remarkably good eye.'"

I once visited Bette Davis at her apartment in West Hollywood, hoping to persuade the very private star to let us photograph her longtime home in New England. She actually agreed, with very little persuasion, picked up a box of kitchen matches, struck one under the table with a great swoop, and lit her cigarette. Wow. She could smoke like no one else ever smoked. She agreed to the feature and I assigned a photographer. At the appointed hour, he was a no-show. That spelled "The End" of the story.

MY SORT-OF INTERVIEWS

In the early nineties two publishers came to Los Angeles to recruit me. Wow, I thought, I'm wanted. That's my weakness. When you are told at a very young age that your mother didn't want you, it plants an insecurity seed that never quite dies. Therefore, it was a delight to hear from a decorator that a top executive would like to come to California and meet with me. Well, *yes*. They certainly weren't coming to me for decorating tips.

Hearst was first. I cannot recall who talked to me. We met in his suite at the Beverly Hills Hotel, where he offered me champagne. There were going to be changes at Hearst, he said, and they would like me to be part of the changes. In fact, "Why not get

on the plane with me tomorrow and work for Hearst? It's time you made your mark in New York." It was one of those times when you later think of what you *should* have said, which was, "Well, I seem to have already made my mark because here you are." I didn't say it, so we talked about nothing much for a few minutes and I said goodbye. As flattered as I was, I declined for several reasons. One, I did not really want to live in New York. Two, I loved working with my wonderful staff. Three, I hated walking alone into an all-new, god-knows-what situation. I couldn't even walk into a cocktail party alone—and still can't.

Some time later Mario Buatta called to ask if I would meet with Si Newhouse, owner of Condé Nast, the next time I came to New York. Of course. We met at his townhouse on East 70th Street. He was direct. He wanted to make editorial changes. Would I come to work for Condé Nast? He said, "You would have a couple of magazines to start, then possibly more, because Alex Liberman will probably retire in a year or so." I replied that it was an amazing offer, but I needed to think about it.

Si: "How long will that take?"
Paige: "A couple of months."
Si: "Can't you think faster?"

I loved him for that, and still do. However, I still did not want to live in New York and walk into what I had heard was a political rats' nest at Condé Nast. So, I wrote what I hoped was a diplomatic note to Si, regretting.

Actually, I didn't regret at all, but there was to be another meeting later with a very different result.

The issue also included several of Katharine Hepburn's homes. ABOVE: Hepburn in Manhattan, in front of a favorite portrait of Spencer Tracy. RIGHT, CLOCKWISE FROM TOP: Comfortable objects filled the living room at her longtime family home in Fenwick, Connecticut. The actress in an African chief's chair that she brought back from filming *The African Queen*. A bedroom cabinet doubled as a hat rack.

ARCHITECTURAL DIGEST

THE INTERNATIONAL MAGAZINE OF INTERIOR DESIGN AND ARCHITECTURE

CHAPTER FIVE

1993-2010

If I Buy the Magazine,
Will You Stay?

The August 2000 "Exotic Homes" cover featured the pavilion
of a house in Ixtapa, Mexico, by architect Manolo Mestre.

ARCHITECTURAL DIGEST

THE INTERNATIONAL MAGAZINE OF INTERIOR DESIGN AND ARCHITECTURE

SEPTEMBER 1996 $5.00

COLLECTOR'S EDITION: INTERIOR DESIGNERS' OWN HOMES

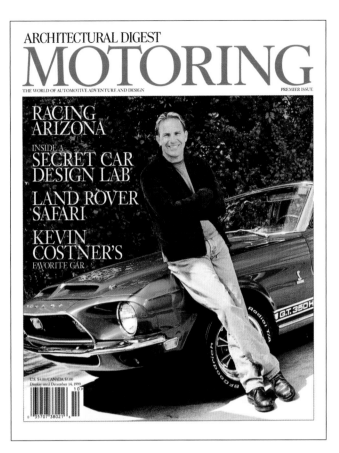

In March 1993 it was announced that Condé Nast Publications had acquired Knapp Communications for a rumored $175 million. Industry executives speculated that Condé Nast Publications owner S.I. Newhouse would position AD as the most elite of his shelter titles in a portfolio that included standouts like Vogue, The New Yorker and Vanity Fair. The editorial offices remained in Los Angeles but the magazine was headquartered in New York City. In 1994 Rense married artist Kenneth Noland and relocated to the East Coast, traveling between homes in Maine, Manhattan and West Palm Beach, with regular visits to the Los Angeles office.

The acquisition didn't bring about major changes to the magazine. Instead, it continued on course, offering the best of the design and architecture worlds. Exclusives included Gore Vidal's villa on the Amalfi Coast, Sir Anthony Caro in upstate New York, Diane Keaton in Beverly Hills, and Katharine

Graham in Washington, D.C. By the late 1990s the magazine tapped its own magnificent history to create special features— AD was often the first to publish many of the designers and architects that are now considered the greatest figures of their fields. In 1999 AD marked the millennium with "100 Years of Design," a monumental, 476-page retrospective that covered the history of twentieth-century design and decoration decade by decade. In 2000 circulation reached nearly 850,000.

Through economic ups and downs, AD remained steady, enjoying a loyal, affluent audience year after year. Subscribers'

LEFT: The residences of, clockwise from upper left, Philippe B. Oates, Mimi London, Mark Hampton and Diane Burn shared the cover of the September 1996 "Designers' Own Homes" issue. ABOVE: "People are the issue," Rense would say. Cover personalities included Ricky and Ralph Lauren at their Double RL ranch in Colorado, left, November 2002; and Kevin Costner and his Ford Mustang on the premiere issue of Motoring, Winter 1999.

letters indicated that they felt as if they were members of an exclusive club. Popular features included Tina Turner in France, Elton John in Windsor, Estée Lauder in Palm Beach, Jean-Michel Frank in Argentina, Robert Duvall's Virginia home (and tango barn), the multiple homes of Ted Turner, Giorgio Armani and Dennis Quaid, Prince Charles' heroic effort to save historic Dumfries House in Scotland, and Michael Bloomberg's restoration of New York landmark Gracie Mansion. As always, Rense welcomed guest writers, among whom were David Mamet, who wrote about his own home renovation near Boston, and Martin Scorsese, who penned stories on Akira Kurosawa and Saul Bass. Proving that past AD stories can be relevant at any time, when Senator John McCain famously couldn't remember how many houses he had during the 2008 election, web traffic for AD's 2005 feature on his Phoenix home soared as journalists sought an answer. (He had eight.)

Shopping and hotel features figured prominently, as did the "AD Revisits" column, which continued to pull from the magazine's immense archive. Set-design features offered special looks at Harry Potter and the Chamber of Secrets (2002) and Something's Gotta Give (2003). The biggest defining factor of the decade was the dominance of special issues: "The Great Design Issue" in May 2003; "Motoring" in January 2004; the "Deans of Design" in January 2005; "The Architecture Issue" in May 2005; and the "Special Design Issue: 100s of Designer Secrets Revealed" in January 2006. New to the magazine was "Open Auditions," an opportunity for designers to submit their portfolios directly to Rense and her staff, with the potential of being published. Rense also returned to books, publishing Hollywood at Home in 2005 and Private Views in 2007. The magazine also published The Literary Collection in 2007, celebrating the contributions of acclaimed writers, including Carl Hiaasen, E.L. Doctorow, John Irving and Derek Walcott.

In March 2010 AD published one of its all-time best sellers, the Jennifer Aniston issue, which sold nearly 120,000 single-sale copies alone. The story followed Aniston's collaboration with Stephen Shadley on the renovation of a 1970s Harold W. Levitt home in Beverly Hills. Just a few months later, in the summer of 2010, it was announced that Rense would retire from the title that she had cultivated into the world's most famous interior design magazine, with more than 850,000 subscribers and a total readership of 5.4 million. She delved into work on the estate and studio business of her husband, who passed away earlier in the year, and moved permanently to West Palm Beach. Her storied forty-year career—the envy of anyone in the publishing world—culminates in this, her twentieth book on architecture and design.

MY NEW BOSS

In 1992 Bud Knapp decided to retire and sell *Architectural Digest*, *Bon Appétit* and a small book publishing division. It was to be an auction handled by Lazard Frères. Prospective buyers would come to Los Angeles to review everything, and I was to do an editorial presentation to each.

I was living in Santa Barbara and commuting daily to the Los Angeles offices but decided to move to the Bel-Air Hotel for the duration. Often, my presentations were followed by lunch with whoever represented the prospective buyer. I was horrified to learn that one magazine publisher divided editorial by percentages. Yikes. I couldn't even figure out what he was talking about, but I prayed his firm was not to be the buyer of *Architectural Digest*. (Its editor, me, could only figure 20% on a lunch check.) During one presentation, I noticed the principal potential buyer was reading a newspaper. Would I have to pole dance to get his attention? After my presentations, there were rarely any questions. I was told that was good but, to this day, I wonder.

Then Si Newhouse came to talk to me in person—a meeting partly arranged by none other than Mario Buatta. Mario phoned and asked if I would meet privately with Si during the *Architectural Digest* auction? Yes, I would. (He was staying at the Bel-Air Hotel, too, so we met in his suite.) I knew Si would ask me lots of questions but his first was a surprise.

Huka Lodge in Taupo, on New Zealand's North Island, began as a fishing retreat in the 1920s and became one of the world's most celebrated hotels under Alex van Heeren. May 1997

204

"If I buy the magazine, will you stay?" I blurted the truth: "I don't know."

I had heard the gossip about Condé Nast and I thought I might be killed if I worked there. "Would I report to you?" He replied, "Yes, but it would mean that we would just have lunch when you were in New York." That sounded promising. "Yes, I would stay." The best answer I ever gave. It resulted in years of professional happiness and friendship with Si and his wife, Victoria, a highly regarded architectural critic and writer (three books and counting). My staff was happy about the change, too. Si spoke to them after the sale and we all agreed that, at last, we had an owner who *loved* magazines.

THE BUSINESS OF ADVERTISING

Legend has it that at *The New Yorker*, advertising people could not board the same elevators with editorial people. That may be apocryphal, and I have not researched it because I want to believe stringent editorial ethics existed once. We had a wonderful advertising director, Tom Losee, based in New York. He respected editorial integrity, so we got on very well for years—until he was asked to retire by a higher-ranking officer. Economics won. Damn. In one way I gladly helped advertisers—by mentioning their products in captions. It seemed courteous. If an interior included an advertiser's product (say, a fabric), then it seemed only right to mention their fabric in a caption, instead of mentioning a fabric by a company that did not support the magazine with advertising. Agreed?

SPOTTING TALENT

In my editor's letter from August 2005, I asked, "Can you guess how many editorial submissions we receive annually? How many within the last year?" The answer? Never fewer than 3,000, rarely more than 4,000. We saw everything. We published very little.

People often asked me, "How do I submit my work for possible publication in *Architectural Digest*?" I thought it had been simple enough, as we received so many by mail, but I decided to announce what we called "Open Auditions," where both professionals and "civilians" could bring photographs of their interiors to our staff. The idea was that we would review everything, and if the home was accepted, it would be photographed and published. It was a terrific chance to discover new designers. But where to hold the auditions? I called Charles Cohen, whom I knew only slightly, and asked him if the auditions could be held at each of the four design centers he owns (New York's D&D Building, DCOTA near Fort Lauderdale, Florida, the Houston Design Center and the Pacific Design Center in West Hollywood). He agreed and, after a few meetings to work out the details, we became friends. And still are.

ABOVE: Virginia Fisher designed the hotel's interior and outdoor spaces, including an alfresco dining area on a balcony off the main room. RIGHT, ABOVE: Guests could charter the hotel's 75-foot yacht, *Sinder.* RIGHT, BELOW: For the saloon, Fisher chose dark blue fabrics to contrast the bird's-eye-maple walls.

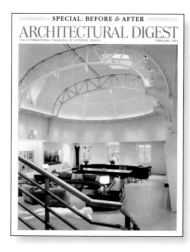

ABOVE: Joan Rivers with her dogs Max, Veronica and
Lulu, in the bedroom of her Connecticut home.
RIGHT: The living room. Rivers hired Joe Cicio to
redesign the house. February 2003

The December 1993 cover caused a scandal. The subject, Barbra Streisand. She is standing in her home next to a painting by Tamara de Lempicka. So far so good. But the painting is of two nudes, male and female. Title: *Adam and Eve*. That was it for some newsstands in different parts of the country. They refused it.

I FELL IN LOVE

On April 13, 1994, *The New York Times* announced my marriage to Kenneth Noland, the internationally collected abstract artist: "A merger of art and architecture: Paige Rense, the editor in chief of *Architectural Digest*, and Kenneth Noland, the painter, were married on Sunday in Mr. Noland's studio in North Bennington, Vt. The couple, who have known each other for 10 years, had intended to keep the guest list small. 'Like many weddings, it started out to be just a few friends, but somehow it grew and ended up close to 60 people,' Ms. Rense said yesterday. The wedding, performed by a justice of the peace, was followed by a dinner at dusk in the remodeled barn that includes Mr. Noland's studio. 'It was romantic, it was magical,' Ms. Rense said, noting that a bit of magic would have come in handy during the final week of preparations. Her administrative assistant, Tanmaya Stoffel, went to Vermont a week ahead of time to help with preparations and came down with the flu. The couple plan to live in New York, Vermont and California, where the magazine's main office is located and where Mr. Noland has another studio. Yesterday, they were both back at work, she in her New York office, he in Vermont. Returning to the job, she said, 'seems easy after doing a wedding.'"

Gore Vidal's Amalfi Coast villa, La Rondinaia—the retreat at which he wrote *Burr*—was published in 1974, a triumph of less is more. About ten years later, we published his apartment in Rome, and Vidal was often asked, "Why there?" His response was, "What

Just off the kitchen was a casual dining and sitting area. Above the fireplace hung a 19th-century French landscape. French doors opened to the terrace and grounds of the 80-acre property.

Rivers chose pink, a favorite color, for her bedroom. The portrait above the fireplace is of the comedienne and her daughter, Melissa Rivers, painted by David Remfry. The white-painted palm trees added a touch of playfulness.

213

THE TWENTIETH CENTURY
ARCHITECTURAL DIGEST
THE INTERNATIONAL MAGAZINE OF INTERIOR DESIGN AND ARCHITECTURE

APRIL 1999

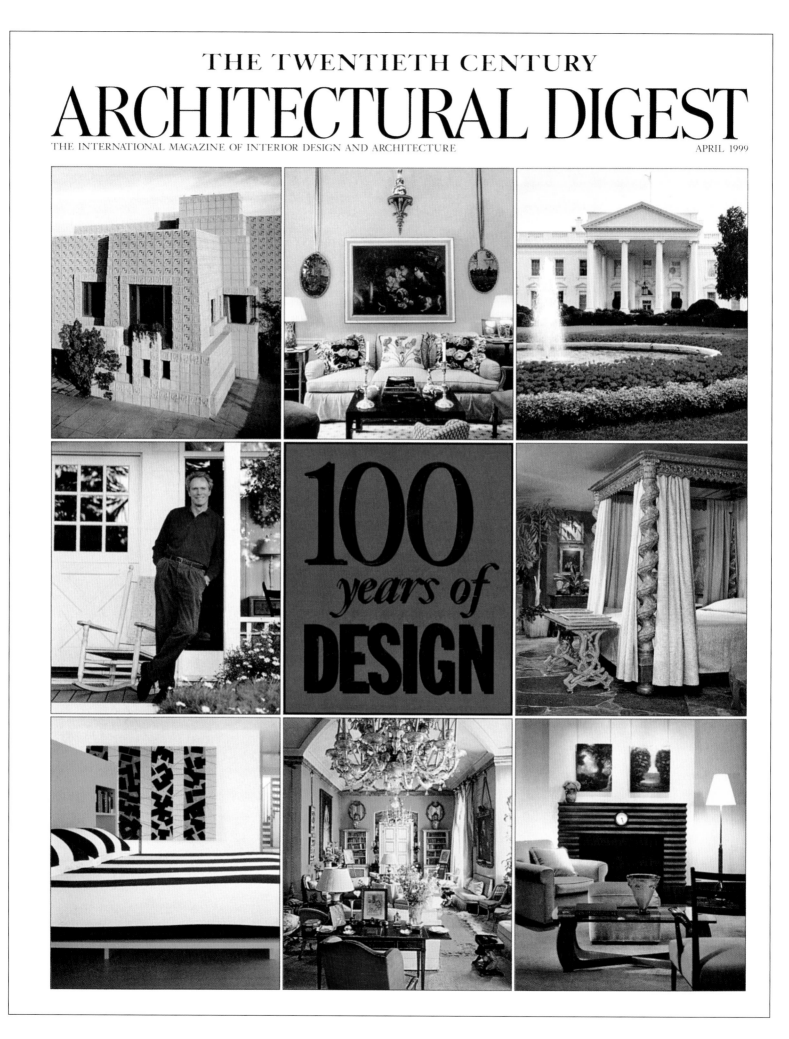

100 years of DESIGN

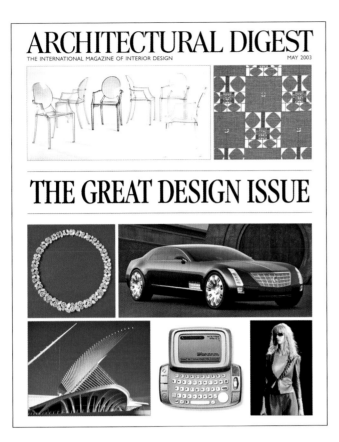

better place to wait for the end of the world than in a city that calls itself eternal." In 1993 he gave up his Roman penthouse apartment and settled full-time into his villa in Ravello, with its eight acres perched a thousand feet above the Mediterranean Sea. When Ken and I were in Todi (we were so enchanted with the town we almost bought a house there), we wired Gore asking if we might visit. He wired back: "Come and stay forever." Ken was deeply involved in making ceramics in Piero Dorazio's studio in Todi, so we didn't. It is a regret.

LEFT: The millennial issue was a decade-by-decade journey through the twentieth century's greatest design moments, pulled from the magazine's archive. ABOVE, LEFT: "The Great Design" issue asked *AD* contributors, architects and designers for their ideas on the most beautiful, practical and clever designs in the world. May 2003. ABOVE, RIGHT: Giorgio Armani on the cover of the April 2002 "New York" issue.

A PLATFORM FOR ANIMAL WELFARE

In 1993 we published wonderful stories on two unlikely subjects, grizzly bears and elephants. The June issue profiled Doug and Lynne Seus, who organized a nonprofit foundation called Vital Ground, which purchases habitats to return to the great bear. It has been said, "If we allow the freedom of the hills and the last of the grizzly to be taken from us, then the very idea of freedom may die with it." I donate to the foundation and perhaps you will, too.

That December we published an article, "Elephants and Interiors," which opened with a photograph of Mark Shand and his elephant, Tara. He wrote the 1991 bestseller, *Travels on My Elephant*, chronicling their 800-mile trek through India. "There is so much we can learn from them and so much to admire, even their pranks. I am besotted with elephants," he told us. Mark, brother of Camilla, the Duchess of Cornwall, wanted to tell the world about the elephant crisis and cofounded Elephant Family in 2002 to help save the endangered

Asian elephant, as well as other animals that share their habitat. I recently returned from Africa, where the killing of elephants for their tusks continues due to eager buyers, primarily in China and Vietnam. Poaching and bribery are still very active, to the shame of we humans.

June 1995 was our "American Country Houses" issue featuring the historic Grey Gardens property in the Hamptons renovated by Sally Quinn and Ben Bradlee. Of the house, Sally wrote, "It was appalling. The roof had caved in, one side of the house was torn off and open to the elements. The porch had been ripped away, the floors had rotted, the antique moldings destroyed, the plaster was peeling, the ceilings and walls were brown with water stains. I was in ecstasy!" Sally Quinn loves saving houses. She is one of the few amateurs who could be a professional interior designer if she ever gave up writing articles, books and reporting.

Candice Bergen was one of our most frequently published celebrities. We began with her home in New York City in 1979, followed by the home she shared with her husband, Louis Malle, in France in 1988. One of their dogs, a Pyrenees sheepdog, slept through our photographic session of the house. Candice explained, "He's on his lunch break, which lasts all day." I first met her years ago in California, although I don't remember how we met. She is totally unpretentious, witty and very good company. She would be welcomed anywhere in the world, even a far

corner of the French countryside. In November 1994 we visited her and Louis again, this time at their home in Beverly Hills. Louis had found the house, which the realtor said was a tear-down. The Malles disagreed and restored it. It was more beautiful than when it was born. Also true of Candice. We featured her, along with dog Lois, on the cover of the issue. Candice designed the home with Karin Blake—two independent, straightforward women who shared a love for simplicity. I like them both. We visited Candice again in October 1999, and again featured her and Lois on the cover, but this time with new dog, too, Larry. "I love Spanish houses—they're the only ones that make sense in Los Angeles," she told us of the hacienda she renovated for herself and her daughter, Chloe, after the death of Louis in 1995. "I don't like houses that take themselves too seriously," she said. "I can only be on my best behavior for so long."

A NEW CENTURY BEGINS

After our first special issue, "The English Country House" in June 1984, many more followed throughout the 1990s. To end the decade, we published "100 Years of Design" issue—our millennium issue—in April 1999. In it, we celebrated a century of design, architecture, interior design and personalities from the pages of *Architectural Digest*, with an introduction of each decade by architectural critic Paul Goldberger. Highlights: *1900s*, Gustav Stickley,

OPPOSITE: Karin Blake designed a Malibu beach house with a New England spirit, pairing a vintage American flag, a 19th-century barber pole and antique jacks in the entryway. January 2008.
FOLLOWING PAGES: French furnishings from the 18th century anchored the living room of Victor Skrebneski's Chicago home. A Gobelins tapestry hung on the far wall, with a painting by Albert Gleizes above the commode. March 2000

Edith Wharton, Theodore Roosevelt, Gaudí, Cezanne. *1910s*, Picasso, John D. Rockefeller, Josef Hoffmann, Frank Lloyd Wright. *1920s*, Mies van der Rohe, James Joyce, Eileen Gray, Rudolf Valentino, Adolf Loos. *1930s*, Katharine Hepburn, Jean-Michel Frank, Le Corbusier, Syrie Maugham, Mondrian. *1940s*, Philip Johnson, Elsie de Wolfe, Jimmy Stewart, Dorothy Draper, Charles Eames. *1950s*, Fornasetti, John Fowler, Dior, Marlon Brando, George Nelson. *1960s*, John Lautner, Kenneth Noland, Andy Warhol, Sophia Loren, Madeleine Castaing, William Pahlmann. *1970s*, Mark Hampton, Michael Tay-

LEFT: An archway to the living-dining room of Joy and Regis Philbin's New York City home. ABOVE: Katherine Stephens designed the space to take full advantage of its Hudson River views. October 2001

lor, Oldenburg, Venturi, Sister Parish. *1980s*, Frank Gehry, Ralph Lauren, Steven Spielberg, Michael Graves. *1990s*, Jed Johnson, Rem Koolhaas, David Bowie, Clint Eastwood and Richard Meier. Among the artists' portraits in this issue are: Miró, Ruscha, Fini, Lichtenstein, Nevelson, Chamberlain, Hockney, Giacometti, Rothenberg, Lartigue, Chagall, Noland, Calder, Morris Louis, Motherwell, Caro. It was a massive and wonderful undertaking.

"Skrebneski Photographs Skrebneski" was a feature in our March 2000 issue on the Chicago home of Victor Skrebneski, written by Aileen Mehle. It was his own home seen through his own lens. One of the most famous photographers in the United States, his spectacular career has spanned fifty years and is still flourishing. He has lived in his Chicago residence, a carriage house, for most of those fifty years. He and decorator Bruce Gregga gently redesigned the coach house to accommodate a studio on the first floor and living quarters on the second. I wanted to send a photographer experienced in shooting interiors. Skrebneski insisted he could do it well himself. He was wrong.

Norman Lear's television series made him a legend—by the mid-seventies, 120 million people were watching at least one of his comedies each week: *All in the Family*, *Sanford and Son* and *Mary Hartman, Mary Hartman*. We first visited him in July of 1992. He and his wife, Lyn Davis Lear (who has a doctorate in psychology), had bought a house in the Brentwood area of Los Angeles and moved in with their art collection: Hockney, Noland, Diebenkorn.

We visited the Lears again in May 2000. Their first design for the house was formal, but with an eleven-year-old son and newborn twin girls, they decided that life had opened up and the house needed to do likewise. Norman observed, "Houses are like writing a screenplay or a movie—you always find things you wish you'd done." For version II of the house, they enlisted decorator Joan Axelrod to express what Norman calls Lyn's "lightness of being." Norman, a longtime art collector, knew Ken before I did and owned several of his major paintings. They became friends, as I did with the Lears at a later date. We are still in close touch, and I continue to regard Norman as a prince who survived the slippery halls of television politics with integrity intact. Norman's autobiography is wonderful. Read it. In our story, he observed of himself, "I'm one of those people who, if I'm having a great meal, thinks it's the best meal I've ever had. I can't imagine a happier place to be."

When I visited the New York apartment of Joy and Regis Philbin, I found an elderly cat on a chair as I was shown through the space. Regis said, "She's blind." I liked them immediately for sheltering and loving an elderly blind cat. When Regis first suggested to Joy that they move from their Park Avenue address to Manhattan's Upper West Side, she immediately saw the benefits for her husband. "The secret to being happy in New York," she said, "is being able to walk to work."

In December 2002 we revisited Wyntoon, a Northern California refuge for William Randolph Hearst. In the 1930s architect Julia Morgan designed several houses as part of his retreat. Its fairytale appearance casts a spell. Begun in the abyss of the Great Depression, Wyntoon was a casualty of that and Hearst's chronic extravagance. Sleeping Beauty House was left a shell with tools, benches and ladders its only furnishings. Attention to physical comfort is one of the memorable aspects of both Wyntoon and San Simeon. Therefore, Wyntoon remains very much a family place, a summer home to serve generations of Hearsts. *Arcitectural Digest* was then, and is now, owned by Condé Nast. I hoped to annoy Hearst's magazine *House Beautiful* by publishing a Hearst house.

In the spring of 2003 we featured Joan Rivers

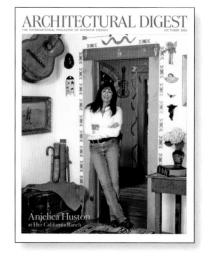

RIGHT, CLOCKWISE FROM TOP LEFT: Anjelica Huston at the entrance to her ranch house, located in California's Central Valley. A corner of her bedroom with photographs Herb Ritts took of her with her dog Minnie. The actress-director found her bed's quilt at a Texas flea market. Production designer Jeremy Railton painting the dining room mural. October 2005

in Connecticut. "This house cost me 214 club dates," she said. "Everything here is a club date." She described the house as she first saw it. "This was the ugliest house I'd ever seen. It looked like a Denny's." She called her friend Joe Cicio, a retail executive, and confessed. He said, "Trust me," and she did. When they were finished with the remodel, the 5,000-square-foot house featured 22-foot-high ceilings, 100-year-old chestnut beams, four wood-burning fireplaces, skylights and a massive country kitchen. In the end, Rivers said she got exactly what she wanted. "This house is about family and close friends sitting around the kitchen table with the fire going, the wine flowing—a place we can be together. When I come here, I bring my own people. I'm a moveable feast." Now she is gone. I knew her—not well but well enough to know that she was down-to-earth and delightful.

WHAT'S MEANT TO BE

In the late 1990s, we debuted *Architectural Digest Motoring: The World of Automotive Adventure and Design*, with Kevin Costner and his Ford Mustang on the cover. I had hoped it would result in another *Architectural Digest* magazine. It didn't. I was disappointed. But we continued to highlight automotive design through special sections called "Motoring," which we first published in January 2004. The following January, we selected 30 "Deans of Design" based on a secret point system devised by the editorial staff. Now I wish I could remove several from the thirty, for very good reasons, but we can't rewrite history.

Sometimes we can have a little fun with it, though. Did you know that very early on, my New York "office" was a hoax? I got so tired of hearing decorators accusingly say, "Oh, you do that California magazine," that I placed the words *New York Bureau* on the masthead, although the bureau did not exist at all. I asked one of our contract writers, the late Peter Carlsen, if we could list him as New York Bureau Chief. He agreed. That was *AD*'s start in the Big Apple. And, as it turned out, quite a good bit of foreshadowing.

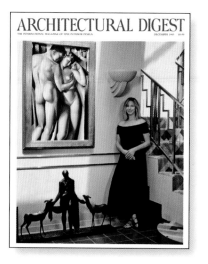

Mark Shand and his wife, Clio Goldsmith, at their home in London. December 1993. Shand, an author and conservationist, went on to found Elephant Family (*elephant-family.org*) in 2002 to help protect endangered Asian elephants and their habitats.

A STARRY NIGHT

An invitation was arranged, a few years ago, to *Vanity Fair*'s Oscar-night dinner. No doubt the arranger was Si. I attended with Ken, who wanted to stand in view of the restaurant's front door and watch the arrivals. At one moment, a hush suddenly came over the restaurant. Muhammad Ali had arrived. I turned to Ken to be sure he had spotted him, but Ken had already stepped forward and was shaking the boxer's hand. At our table, Tony Curtis was on my right. When I told him the man across the table was my husband, a famous artist, he said, "I'm an artist, too." He pulled over the small souvenir *Vanity Fair* notebook that was at each place and drew something. Then Ken drew something on his souvenir book. Dueling artists. But in my opinion, no artist of the time was as great as Kenneth Noland.

THE SMITHSONIAN CALLED—I ANSWERED

In 1990 I began a series of design seminars at the request of the Smithsonian in Washington, D.C. The program, for Smithsonian members who paid admission, began as a six-part series, one session each week. It was a sell-out!

To my delight, the series also caught the attention of some very notable figures and I received the following letter from then-First Lady Barbara Bush:

Dear Paige Rense,

How good to learn that Architectural Digest will be sponsoring a series of lectures about interior design for The Smithsonian Institution. I was especially pleased to hear that the first, very distinguished speakers will be Mark Hampton and Arnold Scaasi, and I know that bodes well for the remainder of the series.

I wish you, Mark, and Arnold the very best of luck on what I know will be a fascinating evening, and I thank you all for sharing your good taste with others.

With all best wishes,
Warmly,
Barbara Bush

CLOCKWISE FROM TOP: The 1877 log cabin of Doug and Lynne Seus, founders of the Vital Ground Foundation (*vitalground. org*), which works to conserve land for grizzly bears and other wildlife in the Northern Rockies. Bart, the Kodiak bear they raised from a cub on the Utah property. June 1993. Mark Shand and his beloved Tara, the subject of his 1991 bestseller, *Travels on My Elephant.*

Every week's program was opened with a few words from me. Then I introduced each designer, who spoke and showed slides of his or her work. Some of the highlights were Valerian Rybar, Renny Saltzman and William Hodgins. At the end of each program, I asked the audience if there were any questions. There were, always. I fielded and apportioned the questions to the designers, trying to make sure each received at least one query.

One program quite a few years later was a surprise hit. In 2004 *Architectural Digest* had shown the Florida home of John Travolta and Kelly Preston, which featured a one-of-a-kind backyard—a landing strip and parking for two huge jets. John was licensed to pilot the big planes and did. He and his lovely wife shared the dais to talk about building and decorating their house—emphasizing views of the jets. At the conclusion, when it was time for the Q&A, hands shot up. There were so many questions by owners of jets that I finally asked if there was anyone in the audience who did *not* own a jet. After the program ended, there was a stampede to the stage. John shook hands, signed autographs and was a perfect gentleman. He and Kelly were both gracious and willing to autograph and talk until I felt a

John Travolta and Kelly Preston's Florida home was designed by architect Dana Smith. Travolta called the pool cabana "a grown-up playroom," as it also offered space for dancing. April 2004

need to intervene, because there was no end in sight. John left his fans reluctantly. No sneaking out a back door surrounded by security. A few months later, when I lived in Maine (and commuted to my New York office), John and Kelly, who had a summerhouse on a nearby island, came to my annual lobster bake. No questions. Just John and Kelly being their charming selves.

Architectural Digest Visits: Anjelica Huston, October 2005. She is on the cover, wearing jeans and standing in the doorway of her California ranch house. On the opening page of the feature, she is wearing a cowboy hat and boots. I like Anjelica, and I thought her 2014 autobiography was well written and fascinating. The ranch, the interior and her animals all add up to one conclusion: Anjelica is the real thing. Looking back on *AD*'s history, it strikes me that famous people let us in because they didn't feel they were inviting millions of strangers into their homes, just fellow subscribers who were their friends. Human beings are natural voyeurs. We all like to see how other people live, particularly celebrities who have become a part of our lives, whether we like it or not.

After purchasing a 1920s Spanish Colonial by architect Ralph Flewelling, Diane Keaton called on her longtime collaborator Stephen Shadley to help restore and redesign the Bel-Air house. November 2008

A GLAMOROUS LIFE?

When I went to a party, it was almost always work. In fact, it seems like my whole life was work. Yet I really liked it that way. I never took a vacation because I didn't know how.

I often found my best leads at parties and would often scout homes myself in the early years. Would you believe I've seen orgy rooms in multimillion-dollar houses? Scouting never really took that long, though. If a house's entry was bad, there wasn't much chance that the rest would get better. But I always went through it anyway. I never made on-the-spot rejections and just tried to be charmingly vague. I didn't like hurting people or making them unhappy. When you reject someone's house, you're rejecting them. My life perhaps hasn't been as glamorous as some people might have believed.

I remember one party in SoHo years ago. The host said, "As editor of *Architectural Digest*, you travel at will all over the world, see the most beautiful homes, are entertained wherever you go, stay in the best hotels, dine in restaurants with stars, fly first class, and your natural habitat seems to be a limousine. You're living everyone's dream. Even Walter Mitty couldn't have fantasized the way you travel." Entire scenes ran through my mind. Quick cuts racing and rolling in reels of Technicolor...

A vintage Bentley comes for me and drives me through rainy Paris streets to designer Jean-François Daigre's house, where, in perhaps the most glamorous room in the world, he and his partner, designer Valerian Rybar, are entertaining a bouillabaisse of titles, wealth and assorted internationals who speak melodiously in six languages, not one of which I understand. Candlelight illuminates faces of the jet set. Chic women in gowns. Mysterious, bronzed men. "No, monsieur, I do not speak French. No, not Italian either. *J'ai regrette*," I say to a man seated next to me on a banquet the size of a Third World nation. Confident because he does not understand me, I smile and speak freely in fluent Candor. "Monsieur, I am a magazine editor. California is my home. I am not rich. My blood is not mingled with that of the Habsburgs, and my dress did not cost twenty thousand dollars. I am neither married to, nor the mistress of, nor heir to one of the world's great fortunes. Monsieur, I'm here on a pass." An ancient hereditary instinct, or perhaps an undisclosed knowledge of English, prompted him to excuse himself with haste.

ABOVE AND RIGHT: The entrance to the home doubled as a library for Keaton's collection of photography and architecture books. Atop the bookcases is stenciled, "The eye sees what the mind knows." FOLLOWING PAGES: Armendaris Ranch, Ted Turner's 350,000-acre wild animal preserve in New Mexico. Turner called on architect Chris Carson and interior designer Laura Hunt to design the hacienda-style retreat. June 2008

The next morning, sipping black coffee on my small terrace overlooking the romantic architecture of Paris, I look over my appointments for the day. I slip the schedule into my handbag and race off to scout three apartments before joining writer Charlotte Aillaud at a restaurant. Just as we finish our discussion, the proprietor approaches. "It would photograph well, the restaurant, no?" "Oh, indeed. But our readers prefer to see residences, monsieur. *J'ai regrette.*" Gripping my coffee, I brace for his next move. "I'm sure your apartment is lovely but I leave for London this evening." I have dodged him, smiling regretfully. "Oh, it's just around the corner? Well, yes, for just a moment." It is just around the corner. Lots of corners. I say no to several thousand homes a year, but I always remain hopeful. The apartment

was filled with boxes, sheets draped over tables. "We close it for the summer when my family goes to Brittany. But you can imagine, yes?" Well, actually, no.

By the time I return to my hotel, I find an irritated photographer pacing the lobby of my hotel. "Americans are always late, yes?" What the hell. "Yes. Always. Let's see your pictures." He has talent. But the pictures are fashion shots. "Have you photographed any interiors, monsieur? No? Well, we could not possibly give you an assignment without seeing how you shoot interiors. No, we don't plan to have a fashion section."

Cursing the decision to wear heels, I totter into the courtyard to meet Michael Taylor, who is in Paris shopping with clients. Michael is charming. His clients are nice. I'm sure their house will photograph beautifully.

At last, I can relax. After all, I have forty-five minutes to wash my hair and dress for the evening. An antiques dealer whom I have never met is giving a dinner in my honor in the apartment he knows I will want to photograph. I had suggested to our mutual friend that I simply stop by and take a look but dinner was *necessaire*. He wouldn't have it any other way. After returning two of ten phone calls, I fling myself into the night.

The apartment is perfectly nice but looks like an antiques shop. It's just not right for the magazine. Interiors are like people. Some are photogenic and some are not. This one isn't. Dinner is three weeks long. Everyone speaks four languages, none of them mine. Finally, the moment arrives. Would I like to see the rest of the apartment? I certainly would not but I do because that is why I am there. He tells me, in suddenly quite adequate English, a little story, *une petite anecdote*, about every object. Overdosed on ormolu, I limp back to the living room wondering if Reebok made a black satin sneaker. Most of the guests have gone home to snuggle under their duvets. "The apartment will make beautiful pictures for *Architectural Digest*, no?" He walks me to the car, his English becoming increasingly crisp. "When will come the photographer?" I apologize and say goodnight.

When I arrive at Heathrow the next morning,

the hotel representative meets me. "It will be your first stay with us? We think it is the most beautiful hotel in London." Oh no. My nerve endings are on red alert. "I am not here to scout the hotel; it is not a business trip at all. We rarely show hotels." Dumb move. "We liked your feature on the New York Ritz-Carlton very much. A lovely hotel. We also enjoyed your feature on the Hay-Adams Hotel in Washington, D.C."

The managing director is waiting to welcome me. Our conversation is an instant replay. For three harrowing days and nights he is stationed in the lobby whenever I try to slip through. On the third morning, I pause for an announcement. "I have seen rooms and suites on my floor while the maids were making them up, and naturally I've seen the restaurant and public rooms."

"Ah, but you've not seen the most beautiful rooms on the top floors! It will just take a moment."

My own law of physics has taught me that there are no moments, only hours. "Of course, if there is time. But I am not here on business," I say, interrupted by the arrival of my next appointment, an interior designer, portfolio in hand. "I'm a little early but I thought you wouldn't mind because, after all, you're here on business." The managing director clenches his jaw, spits out, "Pleasure," and turns on his heels.

OPPOSITE: Ted Turner in the courtyard. ABOVE, CLOCKWISE FROM TOP LEFT: The entrance to the house. The property was developed to raise buffalo and to provide sanctuary for threatened species, including bighorn sheep and Bolson tortoises. The dining room emphasized views and included artworks by George Catlin. Pronghorn antelope also called the ranch home. Turner founded the Turner Endangered Species Fund in 1997. *tesf.org*

At the end of the trip, I settled into my TWA flight bound for LAX. I sighed with delight over the blissful hours of peace ahead of me. Time for leisurely notes. A movie I haven't seen. A new Dick Francis novel. No one can get to me for hours.

"Hi, there! I guess we'll be flying together so I might as well introduce myself. I live in Los Angeles." My seat neighbor stuffs a shopping bag under the seat in front and notices my startled glance at swatches of fabric spilling out. Swatches! "Oh, those are my selections from Colefax & Fowler. Aren't they gorgeous? I'm a decorator; what do you do?"

"Ummm... well...."

"I'm Susan, your flight attendant. And you are..." she consults her clip board. "Paige Rense."

My seatmate turns into the Cheshire Cat. He smiles. He vibrates. He purrs. "You're the editor of *Architectural Digest*! And can you imagine, I almost packed my portfolio but decided to put it in my carry-on. I can show you pictures. I mean, we do have hours and I've seen the movie. Michael Caine is the killer."

I could not wait to be home.

Elton John purchased Woodside, a historic house in Old Windsor, near London, in 1975. Andrew Protheroe and Adrian Cooper-Grigg restored the 18th-century orangery, furnishing the salon with Chippendale settees and old-master paintings, including a portrait by Charles Le Brun above the lamp. FOLLOWING PAGES: Rosemary Verey and Sir Roy Strong contributed to the garden's design over the years. May 2000.

ARCHITECTURAL DIGEST

THE INTERNATIONAL MAGAZINE OF FINE INTERIOR DESIGN

NOVEMBER 1980 $3.50

CHAPTER SIX

At Home with the Editor

Rense's Beverly Hills house, done with architect Jerrold Lomax and designer
Sally Sirkin Lewis, appeared on the cover of the November 1980 issue.

ithout readers knowing it, Paige Rense published three of her own homes during the 1980s and 1990s. The features ran anonymously to ensure that their focus remained on the designers and architects involved, not the resident. The homes (in Beverly Hills, Santa Barbara and New York City) document different times in her life and offer a fascinating glimpse into the private world of the woman behind Architectural Digest. Her Palm Springs home and the home she shared with her husband, artist Kenneth Noland in Port Clyde, Maine, have never been published—until now.

BEVERLY HILLS, NOVEMBER 1980
Tailored to Success
A Vital and Comfortable Setting for a Woman Executive

Surprise. That was my own house on the cover of the November 1980 issue, although it is identified only as the house of a businesswoman. That was me. The house I purchased was very contemporary and rather rigid—a Beverly Hills contemporary with glass walls on three sides and a spectacular view of the city below. It was more the house of the Editor-

In the entrance hall were a pair of 19th-century Cambodian lacquered ponies and antique Chinese *sang de boeuf* porcelain vases. A series of Frank Stella prints can be seen through the doorway.

244

"The decorator you select says a lot. I never chose autocratic designers—the kind who come in and throw everything out, saying 'do what I say.' That's checkbook decorating and reveals that you probably have no interest in your environment."

in-Chief than me. I turned it over to Sally and she made it a house for the Editor-in-Chief and also me. Somehow. I wanted the house to be a place where I could kick off my shoes and relax with friends and for it to be as maintenance-free as possible. Sally created a design that let the living, dining and sitting rooms all flow together, and a bedroom that was as sophisticated as it was feminine. I published the house because Sally did such a great job. It deserved to be seen.

Muted color and expansive glass walls endowed the living room with a feeling of spaciousness. A Thai bronze bust, an 18th-century celadon charger and a jade reclining horse contributed an Asian serenity, while rush rugs and bamboo curtains added texture.

LEFT: Jud Fine's pole constructions joined oak chaise longues in a corner of the sitting room. ABOVE: The master bedroom's subtle gradations of color were chosen for tranquility. The four-poster bed, upholstered in silk and satin, was placed against a bronzed-mirrored wall. Bamboo shades diffused natural light while admitting views of the garden.

"The more you think of yourself, the better your bedroom will be. We spend so much time in them. I sleep, work, read... everything in mine. And I still like those fans in the window."

ABOVE: The dining room of Rense's Palm Springs home, which she designed with Steve Chase. Pink-upholstered fauteuils encircled an intimate table for four. LEFT: A whimsical fan shade joined Don Loper's famed banana leaf wallpaper, Martinque, in the master bedroom.

PALM SPRINGS (UNPUBLISHED)

I bought a condo at the Palm Springs Racquet Club in 1980 because a friend lived there, and it was a good get-away from Los Angeles. The resort had a wonderful history. It was founded by actors Charlie Farrell and Ralph Bellamy in 1934 and was made famous by stars like Bing Crosby and Judy Garland. The residences weren't added until the 1960s— done by developer Paul Trousdale and architect William Cody. I never published the home, even anonymously, because I only had it for a short time. Steve Chase, who lived nearby, helped me with the interiors. We published his work many times over the years, and he had become a friend. I like houses that invite you in with their warmth and livability, so we designed the interiors with comfort and color in mind. Rooms are for people. They should be

The living room featured the bright, cheerful color palette popular at the time. The seating group centered on a Mimi London wood table with a painting above the sofa by Don Sorenson.

"In the end, taste is suitability, the hardest lesson to learn."

comfortable. I think color can help everyone's emotional stability, too. Looking back at the images, the design still ticks a lot of my boxes: simple lamps (chandeliers aren't one of life's necessities) and upholstered dining chairs that let everyone relax in comfort after dinner. My favorite evenings have always been having a few friends over, putting together an easy little dinner and sitting around, talking.

The guest bedroom was done in comforting shades with accents of blue and chrome. A playful koi print was chosen for the rattan side chair. The painting is by an unknown artist.

"You look down a creek to the sea, and there are dogs playing on the shore and children throwing balls."

SANTA BARBARA, SEPTEMBER 1991
Country Spirit on the Coast
A Sun-Washed Setting for Folk Art in California

Surprise again. Leafing through the pages of the September 1991 issue, and there is the Santa Barbara house I loved—and sold only when I married Kenneth Noland, the artist I loved, who lived and worked on the East Coast. The overall plan was to convert a dull, rectangular box suggesting a beach motel into an open-air, lighthearted beach house. I worked with Marc, and when it was completed, I liked it so much I made it my one and only home, along with my dog, Ben, and my folk art. I wish I had them all back, along with Ken. I had painted the floors sky blue and the cabinets yellow in a tribute to the area's former incarnation as a banana farm.

ABOVE: Marc Appleton transformed a 1950s Monterey-style house into a loftlike space for Rense. Eric Nagelmann designed the landscape.
RIGHT: Over the fireplace was a circa 1920 barn-siding painting of a cat. FOLLOWING PAGES, LEFT AND RIGHT: A brass fish was suspended from the beamed living-dining area on the second floor. An antique quilt hung in the dining area.

"I didn't want to live in a 'statement.' I was moving from Beverly Hills, and all I wanted— all!—was a simple house. One reason I turned to Marc was that he understood that."

Every weekday I commuted to my office in Los Angeles and back. It was worth the long commute to come home to Ken, if he was in town, and to walk Ben on the beach. "It's what I really wanted," I was quoted as saying in the article. "A country feeling on the beach. Country but not rustic. Clean lines and contemporary spaces."

PRECEDING PAGES: The master bedroom was hung with paintings by Douglass Parshall, Henri Gilbert de Kruif and Marion Kavanagh Wachtel. Beside the bed was a flower painting by Clarence Hinkle. Antiques included mounted fish decoys, a rocking chair and a 1920s windmill whirligig. RIGHT: Chalkware ducks and skunks occupied a deck off the dining area. The Adirondack chairs were found in Connecticut.

262

ABOVE: A Matisse sketch adorned the entrance hall of the Manhattan home Rense shared with her husband, Kenneth Noland. OPPOSITE: Robert Bray and Michael Schaible turned the East Side apartment into a clublike space. Custom leather-upholstered pieces and a wool-and-sisal carpet gave the living room a sartorial sophistication.

264

"I told the designers that the last thing we wanted was a major construction project—paint it, furnish it, move in. But then, it had to be the right paint, the right furniture..."

NEW YORK CITY, FEBRURARY 1997
Night and Day
Investing Stark Spaces with Urban Style in New York

A New York apartment for an abstract artist and his wife appeared in the pages of the February 1997 "Before & After" issue. Well, wife was me. I asked Bob Bray and Michael Schaible to design an interior in an uninteresting high-rise building overlooking the East River. Ken looked once at the view and said, "We'll take it." For him, the view was all. Other than that, a chair and a bed would be enough, along with, of course, an art studio. For me, a hotel was fine. As I said (anonymously) in the article, "We'd always loved staying in hotels in New York, so when we got our own place there, we wanted to stick with the same kind of carefree anonymity and we went for the hotel mode. You don't have to make everything a nest— now and then it can be more stimulating to 'check in' to an impersonal place, where you're not prompted by the same old trappings to think the same old thoughts." (I did bring a few things from my previous home, though. On one shelf, I can see the Abrams book of Kenneth No-land's work that I had bought before I ever met him—in Santa Barbara, by the way.) Bob and Mike worked out an apartment, all view and much like a clubby hotel suite. The interior worked very well for us: softly tailored ano-nymity. We left after a year, maybe two. As I recall, we moved our city residence to a hotel. Room service.

The thirty-fourth floor offered expansive views. The long table was designed for dining or working.

266

Built on the Maine coast in 1900, the former sea captain's house was home to Rense and Noland for nearly a decade. Earlier in its existence, it had been home to Buddhist monks who built a prayer house in the woods.

The living room included furnishings from the couple's previous homes, like Noland's collection of Navajo rugs and the ottoman and armchairs from their New York City apartment. Native American dolls lined the mantelpiece. To the right hung Noland's *Mysteries: Gold Silence*, 2002.

PORT CLYDE, MAINE (UNPUBLISHED)

When Ken and I married, he had a home and studio in Vermont, but I really wanted to find a place where we could start fresh—no past associations. Friends encouraged me to visit Maine because of the great antiquing, so I went. I fell in love. I found a compound in Port Clyde, a little lobster fishing village, that included an old sea captain's house, two guesthouses, a painting studio and plenty of storage and exhibition space for Ken's work. We purchased it in 2001. Lucky us, it only required minimal remodeling. We didn't know it at first, but we had landed in Wyeth country, and we became friends with Jamie and Andrew, who lived there seasonally. Ken had no interest in interiors, so I was free to choose the things I liked. I brought my collection of folk art, as well as a few pieces from our New York apartment, but we found a lot of charming antiques at country auctions. But it was Ken's work that filled the home. My favorite room was our bedroom, where I had a bay window overlooking the water, a comfortable reading chair, my books, my desk and Ken's art. I was in Manhattan all week and would come up for long weekends with Ken and our friends. Ken passed away in the house on January 5, 2010. I kept it until 2012, when I decided to live full-time in West Palm Beach, Florida.

"Maine is really *away*. It's far from any kind of pressure."

ABOVE: Over the family room fireplace was an untitled handmade paper work by Noland. His untitled silkscreened chevron was to the right. RIGHT, ABOVE: The dining room featured two circle studies by Noland over the mantel, a David Smith ink-on-paper, and another of Noland's paper works near the lamp. RIGHT, BELOW: The writing and reading corner of their bedroom.

I was not aware of *Architectural Digest* in my younger years until it came into being under Paige Rense's direction. She came to New York City, introduced herself and had a dinner for a few of us designers. Shortly thereafter, she featured my work in the November-December 1974 issue and the rest is history. I found myself listed in the inaugural AD100, and I also found myself included in the 30 Deans of American Design. Such an honor. The golden years, indeed. —*Thomas Britt*

The living room of an apartment at the Dakota, November-December 1974

276

I owe my career to Paige Rense. She published many of my projects, which had a minimalist approach to design. Paige had a passion for American folk art, which I collect and use in many of my interiors. I will forever miss the *AD* she created.

—*Karin Blake*

Being a part of the AD100 during Paige's tenure meant everything to me! When my friend and mentor—the late, great designer Kalef Alaton—passed, I was left finishing a project we had started together. It also left me to start Marjorie Shushan Inc. *Architectural Digest*'s stamp of approval under Paige and my inclusion on this list of 100 gave me so much credibility and a platform to showcase my work year after year. Interior design was a gift that came to me later in my life when I was already approaching "a woman of a certain age" status. And the AD100 became something that not only defined my business—it became a part of who I am and something that I am very proud of to this day.

—*Marjorie Shushan*

Being included on the AD100 list solidified our position in the world of interior design. Clients, vendors and companies we work with took note, and overnight we had more respect and authority. We were the same office working to make relevant and beautiful interiors, but the world looked at us differently, and, because of that, we were exposed to more clients who used the list to interview designers for their projects.

—*Thad Hayes*

In 2000 I was lucky enough to be included in the AD100. I felt I had won the equivalent of an Oscar. I was awed and grateful to be awarded the highest accolade in my profession and to be part of an exclusive club that included such titans of design as Mario Buatta, Albert Hadley, Mark Hampton, Juan Pablo Molyneux and Robert A.M. Stern.
—*Elissa Cullman*

The living room of a home in New Jersey's horse country, October 2009

I have been lucky enough in my career in architecture to have had several good turning points. One of them was being recognized by Paige Rense in the many articles and publications of our work. Inclusion in the magazine's coveted AD100 and then the Deans of Design was one honor after another, and I am extremely grateful to Paige and the editors for the opportunity.

—*Hugh Newell Jacobsen*

A Nashville, Tennessee, residence, May 2005

Having been in this business for 40-plus years, I thought the pinnacle would be working with my incredible clients on such amazing projects. But being included in the AD100 amongst such esteemed colleagues truly took my career to its fullest. Paige's recognition—first to publish our work and then to continually include my firm in such a prestigious group—is such a testament to her loyalty and belief in my craft. Being part of the AD100 was, at first, humbling, as I still think of myself coming from a small town in Michigan to New York. Paige's continued support propelled us into a different league. It has been an honor to be recognized, and I have nothing but gratitude to Paige and *Architectural Digest*. The friendship that resulted with her over the years with our numerous collaborations has been a bonus.

—*Mariette Himes Gomez*

The designer's New York City home, September 2002

Other than the recognition from the design world and the general public, the importance of being a participant in this list is a strong personal achievement. I felt like I was being given a title, and the fact that for so many years I have been selected for the AD100 proves that my title is a significant acknowledgment of my work.   —*Juan Pablo Molyneux*

For over twenty-five years, from the publication of our country cottage in the early eighties until our swan song as AD100 architects in 2010, we enjoyed a special rapport with *AD*, from its editor to the entirety of its L.A. staff. These years were the heyday of the magazine, when the world-renowned architectural historians such as Vincent Scully and Joseph Giovannini wrote substantial articles about the homes of "ordinary" people designed by a coterie of influential designers. It was a time when the magazine lived up to its name, *Architectural Digest*. The projects published were eclectic—some contemporary, some classical, some with elegant furnishing and some not—but in every case the quality of the architecture was the dominant raison d'être.   —*Stanley Tigerman and Margaret McCurry*

The AD100 list was a great addition to *Architectural Digest*, as every year we waited eagerly to see if we would have the chance to be listed with the best, to receive confirmation that we were in the game.   —*Mica Ertegün*

The AD100 was a revolutionary way of honoring the best design talent and recognizing each designer as a star. It inverted the usual presentation of a project where the client was featured, even though the reader would generally never see them again. The AD100 made celebrities out of the architects and designers, which elevated them to the artistic level they deserved as creators of worlds in which their clients dwelled. How was this done? By fiat and proclamation, by Paige's vision, without marketing surveys and business consultants.
—*Alexander Gorlin*

A Hamptons beach house, October 2009

Paige revolutionized interior design magazines by rightfully claiming responsibility for many "firsts" in the industry, including the AD100 and Deans of Design lists. Paige transformed the public's perception of architects and interior designers from being regarded as secondary professionals into more influential mainstream icons. — *Geoffrey Bradfield*

PREVIOUS PAGES: The designer's New York City townhouse, September 2005

I first appeared in *Architectural Digest* in 1979, not long after Paige Rense had become editor. I had invited her to view an apartment for which I had designed the architectural detailing and decoration and formed a collection of English antiques as a background for the client's rather important Impressionist art. When Paige was announced, I met her at the elevator and escorted her through the apartment. At least as I remember, she never stopped, hesitated, offered any revealing expression or said one word of any kind. I was simply terrified! I walked her back to the elevator and couldn't resist asking if she thought my work had any merit. As the elevator doors were closing, she replied, "If I didn't, I wouldn't be publishing it."

This was really the beginning of a working relationship spanning over thirty years. It was never discussed, but I instinctively knew that I was to show my work exclusively in *Architectural Digest*, something like being under contract with a major Hollywood film studio. I was always very loyal and, that being said, Paige was always more than loyal to me. Years later, the late S.I. Newhouse asked me why I wasn't afraid of Paige. I told him that she had always been a friend to me and I trusted her judgment without question. He then confided to me. "I'm only afraid of two things in life—one is air travel and the other is Paige Rense."

When Paige retired, I felt the "golden age of decoration," at least during my lifetime, had officially passed. For many reasons, our industry has so changed that it is almost unrecognizable to me, which is probably why I've not submitted any of my projects to any publication since Paige's retirement. I'm certain this is also partially out of my respect for Paige and the many years we worked together. — *Craig Wright*

The living room of a Beverly Hills home, April 2005

The amazing career that I enjoy today was ignited by an invitation from Paige, many years ago, to join her for lunch at the Jockey Club in Washington, D.C. She had seen one of my projects and wanted to meet me. I cannot remember what we ordered, but I do remember the excitement I felt as a young designer sitting across the table from this legendary editor and hearing her lovely words of support. Soon after that lunch, my first project appeared in the pages of *AD*. Paige's constant belief in my work empowered me with the confidence and the opportunities to focus on my own personal design vocabulary. Presently, my firm is involved in design projects around the world, product licensing for major American companies and has developed a strong voice in the design communities both national and international. The value of my relationship with Paige and *AD* has been immeasurable, and its effects seem to be without end. —*Thomas Pheasant*

The designer's pied-à-terre in Paris, February 2003

I was extremely surprised and proud to be included in the AD100 and the Deans of Design. To be in the company of such important and talented designers and architects is an honor I will always remember. —*Sally Sirkin Lewis*

A Bangkok penthouse, January 1987

Paige Rense revolutionized both the publishing industry and the design world during her tenure at *AD*. The publication became the prominent platform for introducing new design and designers to the public, and it became synonymous with the best that the field of interior design had to offer. Without her, I, and many other well-known designers, would not have had that wide-reaching window to showcase our work to the world. She gave me that opportunity, and all those later opportunities throughout the years, to show my talent to people everywhere, and for that she has my everlasting gratitude. —*Juan Montoya*

ABOVE: A family retreat in the Dominican Republic, August 2005; LEFT: An apartment on Manhattan's Fifth Avenue, February 2000

In 1990 I was working with business partner Richard Gillette. Paige Rense first published two of our projects that year in *Architectural Digest* and included us in the very first AD100! It was the beginning of an enduring relationship with AD and Paige. I went on to establish my own practice in 1994, and, in the years since, I've had the good fortune to be included in every AD100. I was on that list before I had a business card, and it continues to be the best calling card in the business!
—*Stephen Shadley*

Jennifer Aniston's Beverly Hills home, March 2010

AD 100 LISTS

Laurence Booth

Fred M. Briggs

Turner Brooks

Theodore Brown

Mario Campi and
  Franco Pessina

Centerbrook

Peter Chermayeff &
  Peter Sollogub

Cicognani Kalla

Stuart Cohen

David Coleman

Steven Conger

Richard Dalrymple

Arthur Q. Davis

Carl Day

Richard England

Arthur Erickson

Joseph Esherick

Frederick Fisher

Florian · Wierzbowski

Frank O. Gehry

William B. Gleckman

Peter L. Gluck

Alexander C. Gorlin

Michael Graves

Graham Gund

Gwathmey Siegel

Steven F. Haas

Hugh Hardy

Cleveland Harp

Agustín Hernández

Arata Isozaki

Franklin D. Israel

Hugh Newell Jacobsen

Helmut Jahn

Charles Foreman
  Johnson

Philip Johnson

E. Fay Jones

Adam Kalkin

Charles E. King

R. M. Kliment &
  Frances Halsband

Edward F. Knowles

John Lautner

Ricardo Legorreta

Michael Mahaffey

William McDonough

Richard Meier

Edward I. Mills

Charles Moore

Moore Ruble Yudell

Morris + Morris

James L. Nagle

Bob Ray Offenhauser

James Olson

John Outram

William Pedersen

Cesar Pelli

Peterson, Littenberg

Barton Phelps

James Stewart Polshek

John C. Portman Jr.

Antoine Predock

Bart Prince

Rob Wellington Quigley

George Ranalli

Horacio Ravazzani

Alex Riley

Jaquelin Taylor
  Robertson

David Rockwood

Paul Segal

David Sellers

Shope Reno Wharton

Lee H. Skolnick

Thomas Gordon Smith

Roy J. Solfisburg &
  Max I. Yelin

Daniel Solomon

Lawrence W. Speck

Robert A.M. Stern

Quinlan Terry

Roland Terry

Tigerman McCurry

Edward Tuttle

Johannes Van Tilburg

Venturi, Scott Brown

Diego Villaseñor

John C. Walker

Warner & Gray

Tod Williams and
  Billie Tsien

Charles T. Young

Marco Zanuso

SEPTEMBER 1995

Ace Architects

Marc Appleton

Arquitectonica

Penny Drue Baird

Javier Barba

Thomas Bartlett

Thomas Beeby

Karin Blake

Laurence Booth

Samuel Botero

Bray-Schaible

Thomas Britt

Bromley Caldari

Anthony P. Browne

Mario Buatta

Diane Burn Bertuzzi

François Catroux

Clodagh

Sibyl Colefax and
  John Fowler

John Cottrell

Robert Denning

Jack Diamond

Diamond & Baratta

Melvin Dwork

Steven Ehrlich

1100 Architect

Joseph Esherick

Toni Facella Sensi

Frederick Fisher

Linda Garland

Frank Gehry

Peter L. Gluck

Alexander Gorlin

Jacques Grange

Michael Graves

Bruce Gregga

Graham Gund

Gwathmey Siegel

Victoria Hagan

Mark Hampton

Hardy Holzman Pfeiffer

Kitty Hawks

Hendrix/Allardyce

William Hodgins

Terry Hunziker

Ike & Kligerman

Irving & Fleming

Arata Isozaki

Hugh Newell Jacobsen

Johnson/Wanzenberg

Jean Jongeward

Robert Kime

Scott C. Lamb

Naomi Leff

Robert K. Lewis

Sally Sirkin Lewis

Mimi London

Timothy MacDonald

Ron Mann

Peter Marino

Margaret McCurry

William McDonough

McMillen Inc.

Mary Meehan

Richard Meier

Sally Metcalfe

David Mlinaric

Juan Pablo Molyneux

Juan Montoya

Moore Ruble Yudell

Olson Sundberg

Parish-Hadley

William Pedersen

Frank K. Pennino

Nancy Pierrepont

Alberto Pinto

Antoine Predock

Jaquelin T. Robertson

Kevin Roche

Aldo Rossi

Serge Royaux

Renny B. Salzman

Harry Schnaper

Stephen Shadley

Shope Reno Wharton

Marjorie Shushan

José Solís Betancourt

Daniel Solomon

John Stefanidis

Robert A.M. Stern

Stanley Tigerman

Christopher Vane Percy

Carleton Varney

Venturi, Scott Brown

Axel Vervoordt

Victoria Waymouth

Bunny Williams

Williams & Dynerman

Paul Vincent Wiseman

Craig Wright

JANUARY 2000

Marc Appleton

Barbara Barry

Karin Blake

Samuel Botero

Geoffrey Bradfield

Bray-Schaible

Thomas Britt

Mario Buatta

Diane Burn

Nina Campbell

François Catroux

Marc Charbonnet

Michael Christiano

Sibyl Colefax &
  John Fowler

John Cottrell

Savin Couëlle

Robert Couturier

Elissa Cullman

Joanne de Guardiola

Alain Demachy

Robert Denning

Melvin Dwork

David Easton

Mica Ertegün

Thomas Fleming

Jacques Garcia

William T. Georgis

Peter L. Gluck

Mariette Himes Gomez

Alexander Gorlin

Jacques Grange

Michael Graves

Bruce Gregga

Graham Gund

Gwathmey Siegel

Victoria Hagan

Nicholas Haslam

Cecil N. Hayes

Thad Hayes

Hilary Heminway

Anouska Hempel

Hendrix/Allardyce

William Hodgins

Terry Hunziker

Ike Kligerman Barkley

Hugh Newell Jacobsen

Greg Jordan

Robert Kime

Rem Koolhaas

Richard Landry

Naomi Leff

Ricardo Legorreta

Sally Sirkin Lewis

Mimi London

Loyd·Paxton

M(Group)

James Magni

Ron Mann

Peter Marino

Margaret McCurry

McMillen Inc.

Mary Meehan

Richard Meier

Juan Pablo Molyneux

Juan Montoya

Moore Ruble Yudell

Mickey Muennig

Philippe B. Oates

Roberto Peregalli

Thomas Pheasant

Nancy Pierrepont

Duarte Pinto Coelho

Campion A. Platt

Bart Prince

Jaquelin T. Robertson

Serge Robin

Serge Royaux

Renny B. Saltzman

Harry Schnaper

Annabelle Selldorf

Stephen Shadley
Shelton, Mindel
Shope Reno Wharton
Marjorie Shushan
Sills Huniford
John Stefanidis
Seth Stein
Robert A.M. Stern
Rose Tarlow
Stanley Tigerman
Edward Tuttle
Carleton Varney
Axel Vervoordt
Verde Visconti
Alan Wanzenberg
Victoria Waymouth
Ron Wilson
Vicente Wolf
Craig Wright
Larry Yaw

JANUARY 2002

Charles Allem
Marc Appleton
Javier Barba
Barbara Barry
Claudio Bernardes &
  Jacobsen
Jeffrey Bilhuber
Karin Blake
Samuel Botero
Geoffrey Bradfield
Bray-Schaible
Thomas Britt
Brown·Davis

Mario Buatta
Nina Campbell
François Catroux
Marc Charbonnet
John Cottrell
Savin Couëlle
Robert Couturier
Elissa Cullman
Roger de Cabrol
Joanne de Guardiola
Alain Demachy
Robert Denning
Dilger Gibson
Melvin Dwork
David Easton
Mica Ertegün
Thomas Fleming
Jacques Garcia
Peter L. Gluck
Mariette Himes Gomez
Alexander Gorlin
Michael Graves
Bruce Gregga
Graham Gund
Gwathmey Siegel
Victoria Hagan
Alexa Hampton
Nicholas Haslam
Cecil N. Hayes
Thad Hayes
Hilary Heminway
Anouska Hempel
Hendrix/Allardyce
William Hodgins
Terry Hunziker
Jaya Ibrahim

Ike Kligerman Barkley
Kazuhiro Ishii
Hugh Newell Jacobsen
Philip Johnson
Greg Jordan
Robert Kime
Richard Landry
Naomi Leff
Ricardo Legorreta
Sally Sirkin Lewis
Donna Livingston
London Boone
M (Group)
Ron Mann
Marc-Michaels
Peter Marino
Margaret McCurry
Mary Meehan
Richard Meier
David Mlinaric
Juan Pablo Molyneux
Juan Montoya
Moore Ruble Yudell
Mickey Muennig
Sandra Nunnerley
Thomas Pheasant
Philpotts & Associates
Nancy Pierrepont
Campion A. Platt
Bart Prince
Jaquelin T. Robertson
Serge Robin
Serge Royaux
Harry Schnaper
Annabelle Selldorf
Stephen Shadley

Shelton, Mindel
Shope Reno Wharton
Marjorie Shushan
Sills Huniford
Michael S. Smith
Scott Snyder
John Stefanidis
Robert A.M. Stern
Stanley Tigerman
Carleton Varney
Axel Vervoordt
Alan Wanzenberg
The Warner Group
Paul Vincent Wiseman
Craig Wright
Larry Yaw

JANUARY 2004

Marco Aldaco
Charles Allem
Marc Appleton
Penny Drue Baird
Javier Barba
John Barman
Barbara Barry
José E. Solís Betancourt
Karin Blake
Samuel Botero
Geoffrey Bradfield
Bray-Schaible
Thomas Britt
Brown-Davis
Anthony P. Browne
Mario Buatta
Marc Charbonnet

John Cottrell
Savin Couëlle
Elissa Cullman
Wallace E. Cunningham
Joanne de Guardiola
Robert Denning
David Easton
Mica Ertegün
Thomas Fleming
Frank Gehry
Peter L. Gluck
Mariette Himes Gomez
Alexander Gorlin
Michael Graves
Bruce Gregga
Frank Grill
Graham Gund
Gwathmey Siegel
Victoria Hagan
Alexa Hampton
Hariri & Hariri
Nicholas Haslam
Thad Hayes
Hendrix/Allardyce
William Hodgins
Kelly Hoppen
Laura Hunt
Terry Hunziker
Ike Kligerman Barkley
Kazuhiro Ishii
Hugh Newell Jacobsen
Greg Jordan
Robert Kime
Naomi Leff
Sally Sirkin Lewis
Donna Livingston
London Boone

Suzanne Lovell
Ron Mann
Marc-Michaels
Peter Marino
Margaret McCurry
Richard Meier
Kathy Merrill
David Mlinaric
Juan Pablo Molyneux
Juan Montoya
Moore Ruble Yudell
Sandra Nunnerley
Thomas Pheasant
Campion A. Platt
Alex Pössenbacher
Jennifer Post
Bart Prince
Jaquelin T. Robertson
Harry Schnaper
Linda Searl
Annabelle Selldorf
Roderick N. Shade
Stephen Shadley
Andrew Sheinman
Shelton, Mindel
Shope Reno Wharton
Marjorie Shushan
Sills Huniford
Michael S. Smith
Scott Snyder
John Stefanidis
Robert A.M. Stern
William W. Stubbs
Rose Tarlow
Stanley Tigerman
Edward Tuttle
Carleton Varney

Axel Vervoordt
Graham Viney
Jack Lionel Warner
Akira Watanabe
Matthew White
Paul Vincent Wiseman
Craig Wright
Larry Yaw
Carlos Zapata

JANUARY 2007

Marco Aldaco
Charles Allem
Marc Appleton
Howard J. Backen
Penny Drue Baird
John Barman
Bill Bensley
Karin Blake
Peter Bohlin
Samuel Botero
Geoffrey Bradfield
Thomas Britt
Mario Buatta
Diane Burn
Timothy Corrigan
Savin Couëlle
Robert Couturier
Elissa Cullman
Wallace E. Cunningham
Joanne de Guardiola
David Easton
Steven Ehrlich
Mica Ertegün
Ferguson & Shamamian
Norman Foster

William T. Georgis
Peter L. Gluck
Mariette Himes Gomez
Alexander Gorlin
Michael Graves
Gregga Jordan Smieszny
Victoria Hagan
Alexa Hampton
Cecil Hayes
Thad Hayes
Anouska Hempel
Hendrix Allardyce
William Hodgins
Kelly Hoppen
Laura Hunt
Terry Hunziker
Ike Kligerman Barkley
Hugh Newell Jacobsen
Jim Jennings
Eddie Jones
Richard Landry
Legorreta + Legorreta
Sally Sirkin Lewis
Donna Livingston
London Boone
Suzanne Lovell
Ron Mann
Peter Marino
Martynus-Tripp
Margaret McCurry
Mlinaric, Henry and
Zervudachi
Juan Pablo Molyneux
Juan Montoya
Moore Ruble Yudell
Katherine Newman
  Design

Sandra Nunnerley
Olson Sundberg
 Kundig Allen
Thomas Pheasant
Campion Platt
Jennifer Post
Antoine Predock
Bart Prince
Jaquelin T. Robertson
Jacques Saint Dizier
Harry Schnaper
Annabelle Selldorf
Roderick N. Shade
Stephen Shadley
Shelton, Mindel
Shope Reno Wharton
Marjorie Shushan
Sills Huniford
Scott Snyder
José E. Solís Betancourt
John Stefanidis
Robert A.M. Stern
William W. Stubbs
Emily Summers
Rose Tarlow
Roger Thomas
Stanley Tigerman
Suzanne Tucker
Mitchell Turnbough
Edward Tuttle
Carleton Varney
Axel Vervoordt
Diego Villaseñor
Graham Viney
Alan Wanzenberg
The Warner Group
Dennis Wedlick

Bennett and
 Judie Weinstock
Paul Vincent Wiseman
Craig Wright
Pierre Yovanovitch

JANUARY 2010

Marco Aldaco
Thomas Allardyce
Charles Allem
Marc Appleton
Howard J. Backen
Penny Drue Baird
Bannenberg & Rowell
Javier Barba
John Barman
Bill Bensley
Marcos Bertoldi
Karin Blake
Count Benedikt Bolza
Samuel Botero
Peter Roy Bowman
Geoffrey Bradfield
Thomas Britt
Mario Buatta
Diane Burn
Candy & Candy
Timothy Corrigan
Savin Couëlle
Elissa Cullman
Wallace E. Cunningham
Joanne de Guardiola
Mark de Reus
Douglas Durkin
David Easton
Steven Ehrlich

Mica Ertegün
Ferguson & Shamamian
Norman Foster
Linda Garland
William T. Georgis
Mariette Himes Gomez
Alexander Gorlin
Michael Graves
Allan Greenberg
Robert M. Gurney
Victoria Hagan
Mona Hajj
Alexa Hampton
Hariri & Hariri
Nicholas Haslam
Thad Hayes
Ann Holden
Laura Hunt
Terry Hunziker
Ike Kligerman Barkley
Hugh Newell Jacobsen
David Jameson
Jim Jennings
Stephen Knollenberg
Richard Landry
Martyn Lawrence-Bullard
Michael Lee
Donna Livingston
London Boone
Ron Mann
Peter Marino
Marmol Radziner +
 Associates
Margaret McCurry
Richard Meier
Miró Rivera Architects
Juan Pablo Molyneux

Juan Montoya
Moore Ruble Yudell
Katherine Newman
Sandra Nunnerley
Olson Kundig Architects
Thomas Pheasant
Mary Philpotts McGrath
Campion Platt
Alex Pössenbacher
Jennifer Post
Antoine Predock
Bart Prince
Chakib Richani
Jaquelin T. Robertson
Jacques Saint Dizier
Nina Seirafi
Annabelle Selldorf
Stephen Shadley
Shelton, Mindel
Shope Reno Wharton
Marjorie Shushan
Michael S. Smith
Scott Snyder
José Solís Betancourt
John Stefanidis
Robert A.M. Stern
Emily Summers
Ken Tate
Roger Thomas
Suzanne Tucker
Edward Tuttle
Wang Ta-Chun
Paul Vincent Wiseman
Craig Wright
Pierre Yovanovitch

JOAN RIVERS

March 21, 1978

Paige Rense
Architectural Digest
5900 Wilshire Blvd.
Los Angeles, Ca. 90036

Dear Paige,

I want to thank you so much for adding a touch
of class to the Mike Douglas Show on the day
you appeared.

We totally enjoyed your book as we oohed and aahed
at the celebrity homes all the way from Philadelphia
to Atlanta. As I told you going over in the car,
we already had a copy of the book, so I quickly
sent it to my sister in Georgia (poor thing) so
that she too could get many hours of pleasure
enjoying it as we did.

Again, many thanks. It was a pleasure meeting
you and I hope that next time I host the Johnny
Carson Show I can have you on along with me.

Most sincerely,

Joan Rivers

THE WHITE HOUSE

April 13, 1990

Dear Paige Rense,

How good to learn that ARCHITECTURAL
DIGEST will be sponsoring a series of
lectures about interior design for the
Smithsonian Institution. I was especially
pleased to hear that the first, very
distinguished speakers will be Mark
Hampton and Arnold Scaasi, and I know that
bodes well for the remainder of the
series.

I wish you, Mark, and Arnold the very best
of luck on what I know will be a
fascinating evening, and I thank you all
for sharing your good taste with others.

With all best wishes,

Warmly,

Barbara Bush

Ali MacGraw

...ely thrille
...ry you did
...roscopic
...sque. And
...flabbergha
...on the cove
...you for alwa
...ing my idiosy
...! I think
...ber of people
...on whether all
...al bracelets, sill
...shelter animals
...ly constitute "st
...re very generous
...thankyou very, ver
...o hope you are w
...: new eng

RALPH LAUREN

October 3, 1986

Ms. Paige Rense
Editor-in-Chief
ARCHITECTURAL DIGEST
5900 Wilshire Boulevard
Los Angeles, CA 90036

Dear Paige,

I wanted to let you know how much I enjoyed our
lunch, and how wonderful I think the article turned
out. Thank you for such a bea... l piece. I
hope you are as pleased with t...

With warm personal regards,

Ralph

Ralph Lauren

RL:acd

S.I. NEWHOUSE JR. 11/28/97

Paige,
I'm proud of AD and
of being your colleague.
Best Wishes
SI

Gianni Versace

October 11th 19

ANSEL ADAMS

ROUTE 1, BOX 181, CARMEL, CALIFORNIA 93923 TELEPHONE (408) 624-2

February 28, 1983

Paige Rense
Editor in Chief
Architectual Digest
5900 Wilshire Blvd.
30th Floor, Editorial
Los Angeles, CA 90036

Dear Paige Rense:

Virginia and I were honored to be asked by your
magazine to have our home in its pages. I do know
that we at first changed our mind and at least
a year passed before we were back feeling positive
about cooperating with you on this. We both
began worrying about possible loss of privacy.
The article is simply beautiful, both the photographs
of Mary Nichols and the words by Connie Glenn.
And - no one could pick out where our house is
along the coast - our privacy is preserved!
I thank everyone for their sensitivity to this.

I do think that the real feel of the house was
communicated. Mary Nichols did such a very fine
job, and she was a delight to have in our home.
She was very professional, took little of our
own time, just went right ahead with her work.
We all liked her very much.

And Connie Glenn has been a friend for a number
of years, as well as a respected colleague.
It was a pleasure to talk with her for this
story. Indeed I look forward to seeing her this
weekend. We serve on the same board of trustees.

So, thank you for your excellent taste in the
people who work for your magazine and thank you
for the excellent taste of the magazine itself.
It was a delightful experience.

Cordially,

Ansel Adams

REGIS PHILBIN

Dear Paige -

Do I really live in this apartment I'm looking at
in your magazine? Is the sky really that blue? Is the
piano that pretty? My God, Paige, it looks fabulous
and your photographer, Durston, is a magician. What a
terrific job he did. And I can't tell you how many people
have mentioned it to me. Forget about Time and People, the
magazine cover to be on is Architectural Digest. We
couldn't be happier with the way it turned out. Thank you
so much. Our Best To you,

Regis & Joy

...actually, it's a loving...
...haven retreat, and graceful as on...
...Come see for yourself, Beverly Hills...

...t your kind letter and
the beautifully bound copy of ARCHITECTURAL DIGEST
which contains the article on our home in Carmel.

It is a distinguished job and we are much pleased!
The photography is supurb! Our home is not easy to
photograph but the pictures...

Letters to the Editor

I didn't know about *Architectural Digest* at all until one of my earlier clients in the late-seventies, for whom I designed a very elaborate pool house/guesthouse in Greenwich, Connecticut, brought the magazine to my attention. In any case, I didn't know about *AD* until the pool house was published in *House & Garden* and my client asked if I knew about *Digest* and why hadn't I considered publishing it there. She obviously was hip to what you were doing before I was. Somewhere in this primordial, dark, cavelike phase of my existence, I did eventually get in touch with you—or you got in touch with me; I can't remember how our first date took place—and I was fortunate enough to have you publish a rather grand apartment on Fifth Avenue in 1983. You put it on the cover, which made me feel great—although I wasn't quite ready to die and go to heaven, that debut in *Architectural Digest* gave me a sense of what it might be like to do so. I was thrilled.

Robert A.M. Stern

As editor-in-chief for 35 years, Paige Rense took what had been a trade journal and created the world's most successful shelter magazine. I'm proud to have had a number of my homes featured in the pages of *Architectural Digest*. Along with her brilliant success, my heart goes out to Paige for her undying love and commitment to the philosophy of people helping animals and animals helping people.

Diane Keaton

Dear Paige,
I'd like to acknowledge the privilege of having been published so many times over the years since 1984 in *Architectural Digest*, as well as being honored as a long-standing member of the AD100 group of designers and architects. I wanted to write and share part of my perspective on why *AD* has been important to my career, and to so many others, too.

Sometimes, long after an article appears, one meets with a prospective client who opens a folder full of magazine clippings, among them not just one but often two or three projects of ours that *AD* has published. This is the client we cherish, a client that *AD* has helped bring our way, and it is why I feel lucky to have had our projects included in the magazine's

pages over the years.
Marc Appleton

In the 1970s *Architectural Digest* started to have a sort of renaissance, emerging from a mostly black-and-white periodical into an all-color interiors magazine. Word spread quickly that it was looking for the best design and designers. Here was a guide for the right of good living, specifically the creation of homes that would serve as the setting where contented lives and stories of success would be reported. At first, the magazine grew fashionable. Later, it became essential. Every successful home, office and business had copies on view. They were symbols of inclusion in the lifestyles being shown. The presentation was a combination of beautiful imagery and friendly text. It got things moving. It gave everyone an opportunity to excel. To have lived and experienced that magical era was a unique privilege.

Jaime Ardiles-Arce

To the Editor,
Since the early 1970s we have always anticipated the monthly arrival of *Architectural Digest*: to see the latest transformation of a home we had known for years; to see what to expect to experience at drinks later that month; to see the newest project of a professional whose work one admired or even valued as a friend; to see the latest acquisition of a noted art collector and how that related to the work already in the collection; to keep up-to-date with emerging trends; to see what might work at home; but most of all, to fantasize how to live life well and comfortably.

Douglas Baxter
Pace Gallery, New York City

When I moved to New York City from London in 1974, I was given my first subscription to *Architectural Digest* for Christmas that year. I loved being a voyeur into the homes of the rich and famous and marveled at what talented people could achieve with a few yards of Fortuny fabric and a lot of vision.

Three of the properties I managed were published in the magazine: The Carlyle, New York City (Mark Hampton); the Ritz-Carlton, New York City (Sister Parish); and Hotel Bel-Air (Robert Zimmer). Not only was wonderful photography involved but many of the writers gave marvelous insights into the lives of the featured people. It was a social history with pictures. Each article was a concise study of a specific place and time. The importance of *Architectural Digest* was incalculable in those pre-internet days, as the magazine was virtually alone in what it was chronicling with interior design. Indeed, the magazine was so important and beloved that many of us could not part with a single back issue.

Frank Bowling, Hotel Ambassador
Montage Beverly Hills

Interior design achieved a new kind of status in the pages of *Architectural Digest*, becoming as integral to one's level of sophistication as the appreciation of art or knowledge of fine wine. These were the years, after all, when the word *starchitects* was coined to describe the towering talents of Frank Gehry, Richard Meier and Robert A.M. Stern, among others. So, too, interior designers became celebrities. It is impossible to overstate the importance of *AD*'s millennial issue, which carried the cover line, "100 Years of Design." No magazine had ever attempted an undertaking of such encyclopedic ambition or, for that matter, has done so since. A 476-page compendium of design history, the issue guided readers decade by decade from 1900 to century's end. Not only did it make the most persuasive case possible for the legitimacy and importance of design through this age, it captured the contours of the extraordinary cultural adventure of the past 100 years. The magazine industry is a very different animal these days. Budgets are smaller, the internet distracts the audience for interior design with more spontaneously attention-grabbing technology. It is impossible for those of us who knew this golden age of publishing not to indulge in a spell of nostalgia.

Geoffrey Bradfield

Dear Editor,
For me, *Architectural Digest* has always been the platinum standard and the go-to guide covering the best residential interior design projects in the world. Whenever I have undertaken a personal design project for a new home, I always familiarize myself with the great design talent found within the pages of *AD*. It is, with-

CAROL BURNETT

January 21, 1997

Dear Paige,

I wanted to thank you for sending me the leather bound edition of the December, 1996 issue of Architectural Digest. It is absolutely beautiful. What a presentation! I truly enjoyed working with you on this so much, and I'm delighted at the results.

Love,

Carol

out doubt, my first stop for inspiration.

Architectural Digest's pictorial production has always been coupled with literary excellence in its reporting. The photography captured within the pages of *AD* has always succeeded in presenting design projects as art, worthy of framing by itself.

Looking back on past issues, one experiences a record of how we lived and what we aspire to as devotees of design. Given *AD*'s reach throughout the world, you will be hard pressed to find a better representation of design talent working today.

Very truly yours,
Charles Steven Cohen

Paige,
I have been a devoted fan of *Architectural Digest* since I was a young married woman and a graduate student in Japanese studies—not yet thinking of becoming a decorator. Each month I raced to the mailbox to see what the magazine was showcasing. The vibrant images of French chateaus, English country houses, rustic retreats, sophisticated Manhattan penthouses and the like were dazzling, and the well-written texts by Susan Sheehan, Gerald Clarke, Brendan Gill and Paul Gold-

berger were illuminating.

But it wasn't until I started my business in 1984 that I realized that *AD* had been, in effect, my graduate school in interior design. *Architectural Digest*'s pages had opened my eyes to the best of national and international interior design and architecture, a private tour of exclusive residences that I would never have had access to. And, when after almost ten years of submitting projects, Paige Rense finally accepted a Nantucket home, I was over the moon—my firm was being recognized by *Architectural Digest*!

I have always used my extensive library of past *AD*s to research projects. The magazine's early standards of excellence have stood, and will stand always, the test of time.

Warmest,
Ellie Cullman

After serving in the Navy and Marines as a hospital corpsman and working as an EMT in an emergency room in Indianapolis, it was time for a career change, so I headed to Los Angeles. Since I knew nothing about L.A. or the job market, I sought the help of a staffing agency for employment. In December 1980 I landed a job in the mailroom at Knapp Communications, owner of *Architectural Digest* and *Bon Appétit* magazines. Although I knew nothing about publishing, or *Architectural Digest* for that matter, in July 1981, I was given the opportunity to join the *AD* team as a graphic assistant. As time passed and my knowledge of the design world evolved, I found myself working closely with photographers on upcoming photo assignments. This provided me the opportunity to interact with decorators, architects and homeowners. Not only was *AD* at the forefront of capturing the design world but it was also photographing kings and queens and other heads of state, along with historic houses, gardens, collections and anything else that piqued the readers' interest, and it worked. I'm grateful for my thirty years with *Architectural Digest*. It was the greatest "E" ticket ride one could envision!

James G. Huntington

I always knew I had the best job working at the best magazine for the best editor, Paige Rense. Yes, she was my boss, but she was also a great friend and a wonder-

ful mentor. I know I share this view with many others. With a sportive look or comment, she could push you beyond your comfort zone. You certainly did not want to disappoint. I remember sitting with a designer, practicing speeches we were to give to a large group. We were petrified. Paige took us aside and said, "They love us. They want to hear what you have to say, so for the next few minutes pretend that you are someone else." We did, and she was right.

People who came to listen and readers who religiously read *AD* were the ones Paige cared the most about. She also cared about her staff and would often tell us that we were "the best magazine staff in the world." Her standards were high and her vision for the magazine was very clear. She encouraged the best work from everyone who worked for her. The lessons learned, the experiences we shared and the pride we took in the work we did still remain, and I am forever grateful.

Margaret Dunne

In the late 1970s I became interested in modern art and over time began collecting. One day, visiting a collection in Pasadena, the daughter of my collector friend told her dad she had spoken with the painter Kenneth Noland and told him her father would have to call him back. "Has he sold the farm?" my friend asked. They hadn't spoken of that, was her reply. Interested in Kenneth Noland as an artist, I asked a question or two and learned that Mr. Noland was selling a farm in Shaftsbury, Vermont. My heart pounded. I loved Vermont, had been thinking of a second home for my family, and knew in that instant that I had found it. I called Noland later that day and learned that he had purchased the property many years before from the estate of Robert Frost. A Robert Frost farm in Vermont!

I purchased the farm from Ken in the mid-seventies, we became fast friends, and, years later, when he fell in love and married Paige Rense, I was introduced to *Architectural Digest*. I loved Paige from the moment I met her, just as I did her husband years before, and over time fell in love with her magazine as well. In 1988 my wife, Lyn, and I purchased a home in Brentwood, California. With the aid of John Saladino, Lyn decorated it. When Paige and Lyn grew to know one another, Paige was curious to see the home Lyn had fashioned for us.

She gasped when she saw it. (A gasp from an *Architectural Digest* editor is an urgent request to include an edifice in the very next edition of her publication.)

And so it was that our now just shy of thirty-year residence appeared in the July 1992 issue. I couldn't know until that occurred what a badge of honor and respect it was to find one's home pictured in that most august of journals. I continue to delight in that all these years later.

Norman Lear

When Paige Rense asked me to write for *Architectural Digest*, I didn't know a Louis IXV from an Herb the 5th. "You understand the psychology of design," said my intuitive new boss. Eventually, I caught on and learned that sophistication was best served up with a wink. John Travolta's sense of fun played out in his own Florida front yard. Adjacent to the private runway, his two planes (a Gulfstream II jet and a Boeing 707 airliner) were parked 100 feet from the front door. Inside, the house was patterned after a '50s air terminal. And who but Cher would plunk an Egyptian Revival palace on a Malibu beach? In the end, *AD* turned out to be a master's degree in design, sociology, architecture, history and human nature. How very lucky was I?

Nancy Collins

When I think about *Architectural Digest*, I think about a magazine that transformed the public's perception of architects and interior designers, giving them a relevant place in the world of creative design and cultural icons. When I write about the magazine, a name naturally flows from my pen, that of Paige Rense. It is impossible to disassociate one from the other, as both are close to me.

Architectural Digest showed us the widely diverse and exciting worlds in which people lived, and it became the undisputed arbiter of style. *Architectural Digest*, a magazine that delights the connoisseur's eye—the bold eye—and stimulates the mind with an intelligent approach to design, has solid roots. These roots were strong and extensive even back in the early eighties, when I was honored with my first publication, a double cover.

Juan Pablo Molyneux

June 24, 1985

Ms. Paige Rense
Editor-In-Chief
Architectural Digest
5900 Wilshire Boulevard
Los Angeles, CA 90036

Dear Paige:

Both Ivana and I want to thank you for the piece you did in ARCHITECTURAL DIGEST this month. The text is accurate, descriptive, and we think your photographer did a magnificent job. The apartment looks absolutely great.

We are very pleased, and very proud, to have our home included in your publication.

Sincerely,

Donald J. Trump

Dear Paige,

So often I have thought of the thirty-plus years I was so privileged to take photos for *Architectural Digest* under your editorship. What more could a photographer ask for? The quality of the design and architecture was a constant source of education for me, and every assignment was another opportunity to do my best for a magazine that was unlike any other. Knowing that you, and a group of people you put together, all had the same vision of communicating what was happening in the world from the very best talent was a tremendous source of support. The layouts were beautiful and the photos used in such a way that they seemed to put the reader right there. In a time now when everything seems temporary, these photos and articles still stand out as a clear statement of what so many aspired to and were inspired by, just as I was and still am.

Thank you,
Mary E. Nichols

Early in my career, I designed in partnership with Richard Gillette. We were young and eager to be published and pursued *House & Garden* because we thought it was "hip." I don't think we ever considered we would be good enough to be included in *Architectural Digest*. It was the gold standard and had an exclusive roster of established designers and architects. In 1989 Paige Rense became aware of our work through one of her editors and invited us to tea at the Carlyle Hotel! We went knowing it was not just another meeting. Paige reviewed our portfolio of work and accepted on the spot two projects for the magazine! In 1990 a spring story on the director Robert Altman and his wife Kathryn's New York duplex appeared and that fall, another feature on a serene Central Park West apartment. That same year, *AD* launched the very first AD100 list and we were included. At the time, we didn't even have a business card!

Stephen Shadley

Dear Editor,
What can I say? The pure truth: that your *Architectural Digest* has been for me an extraordinary school of work and life. In 1980 my publisher, Giorgio Mondadori, called me and said, "Here's the magazine we should create," showing me a copy of *Architectural Digest*. He was thinking of creating a magazine dealing with furniture, but with the glamour of *Domus*, *Casabella* and *Casa Vogue*. Giorgio and I arrived in the U.S. to meet with you and discuss the project. It was the first of many enlightening meetings. We needed, as you explained to us while turning the pages of *AD*, houses linked to a contemporary point of view but that included both classic and modern furnishings, which should be photographed with an eye-catching look. This was a memorable lesson, and through the years, I've learned to have no stylistic prejudices; modern is as significant as classic, eclecticism is as good as minimalism; taste makes the difference. Over time, our meetings became friendlier but not without an occasional confrontation and reflection. As you were providing suggestions on how to avoid mistakes, I was trying to catch as many "secrets" as possible from you. I felt we were a real team; our work relationship had become trusting, along with our friendship, a true friendship that lasts today. Thank you, my dear editor and friend.

Ettore Mocchetti
Editor-in-Chief, AD Italia

Architectural Digest gave a bird's-eye view of the most celebrated homes in the United States and abroad. In my office, I still have very old issues, and I can see the changes over the years, following the world's appreciation of decorators from an unrecognized state to stardom. The decorators, now interiors designers, were challenging themselves to capture Paige's sharp eye to receive the recognition of *Architectural Digest* by having a project published. The magazine was able to show the ideas of many designers to its readers to enlighten their views of modern living. Paige brought her artistic sense to the magazine—a valuable addition to her journalistic skills—and with her dedication, *Architectural Digest* was transformed into the most prestigious reference in interior design.

Mica Ertegün

Dear Editor,
As two people who have a strong interest in architecture and design, we have always admired *Architectural Digest* and its commitment to forwarding the integrity of design as an art form.

We have always been able to count on *Architectural Digest* to feature a wide variety of architectural styles, reflecting the wide array of viewpoints in the field. The true appreciation and respect for different styles of design is apparent throughout every article.

Architectural Digest featured two of our homes, one in Florida and one in Maine. We greatly appreciate the care the magazine took in telling the story of each property. The features were able to capture the homes beautifully and communicate the exact aesthetic and character of each space. As a result, the readers were able to see how it would really feel to be there. This same feeling is captured in each issue, leaving readers truly inspired to create their own incredible spaces.

Thank you for your continued work to share design with the world!

John Travolta and Kelly Preston

There will never be another.

After her retirement in 2010, Paige Rense was given the title of Editor Emerita of *Architectural Digest* and remains on the masthead today.

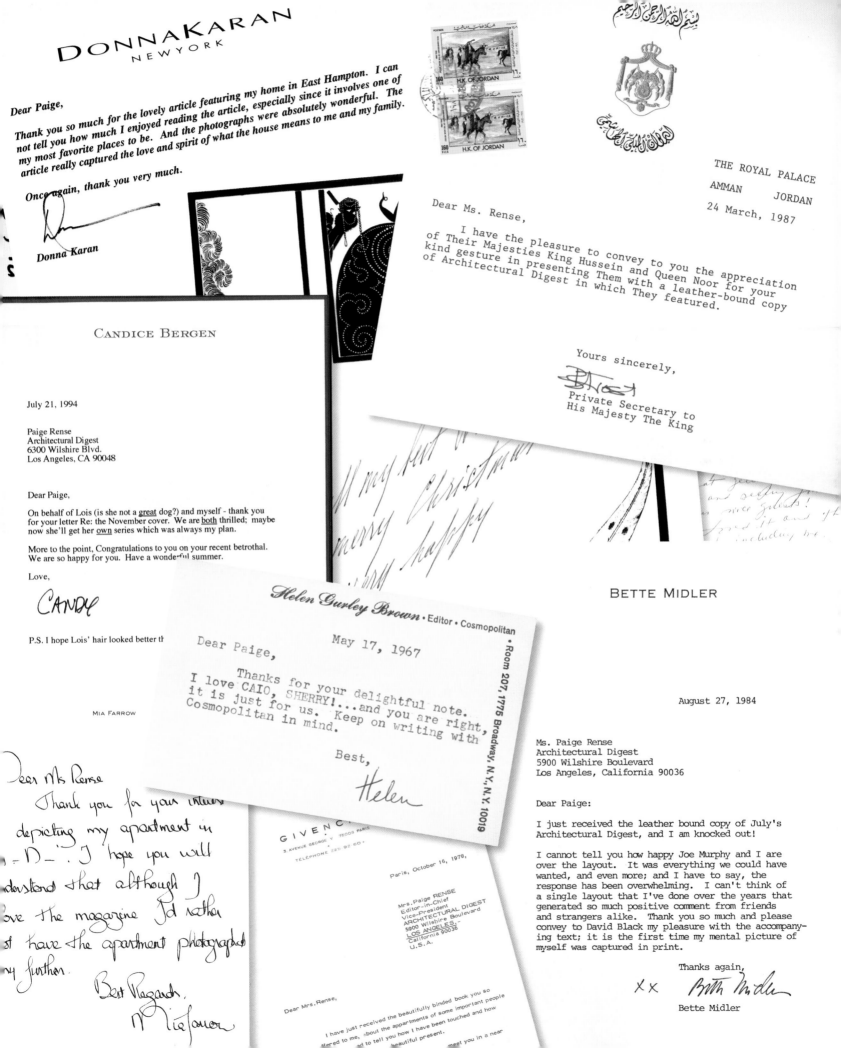

DONNA KARAN
NEW YORK

Dear Paige,

Thank you so much for the lovely article featuring my home in East Hampton. I can not tell you how much I enjoyed reading the article, especially since it involves one of my most favorite places to be. And the photographs were absolutely wonderful. The article really captured the love and spirit of what the house means to me and my family.

Once again, thank you very much.

Donna Karan

THE ROYAL PALACE

AMMAN   JORDAN

24 March, 1987

Dear Ms. Rense,

I have the pleasure to convey to you the appreciation of Their Majesties King Hussein and Queen Noor for your kind gesture in presenting Them with a leather-bound copy of Architectural Digest in which They featured.

Yours sincerely,

Private Secretary to
His Majesty The King

CANDICE BERGEN

July 21, 1994

Paige Rense
Architectural Digest
6300 Wilshire Blvd.
Los Angeles, CA 90048

Dear Paige,

On behalf of Lois (is she not a great dog?) and myself - thank you for your letter Re: the November cover. We are both thrilled; maybe now she'll get her own series which was always my plan.

More to the point, Congratulations to you on your recent betrothal. We are so happy for you. Have a wonderful summer.

Love,

CANDY

P.S. I hope Lois' hair looked better th

BETTE MIDLER

August 27, 1984

Ms. Paige Rense
Architectural Digest
5900 Wilshire Boulevard
Los Angeles, California 90036

Dear Paige:

I just received the leather bound copy of July's Architectural Digest, and I am knocked out!

I cannot tell you how happy Joe Murphy and I are over the layout. It was everything we could have wanted, and even more; and I have to say, the response has been overwhelming. I can't think of a single layout that I've done over the years that generated so much positive comment from friends and strangers alike. Thank you so much and please convey to David Black my pleasure with the accompanying text; it is the first time my mental picture of myself was captured in print.

Thanks again,

X X   Bette Midler

Bette Midler

Helen Gurley Brown • Editor • Cosmopolitan • Room 207, 1775 Broadway, N.Y., N.Y. 10019

May 17, 1967

Dear Paige,

Thanks for your delightful note. I love CAIO, SHERRY!...and you are right, it is just for us. Keep on writing with Cosmopolitan in mind.

Best,

Helen

MIA FARROW

Dear Mrs Rense

Thank you for your interes
depicting my apartment in
_D_. I hope you will
_derstand that although I
ove the magazine I'd rather
t have the apartment photographed
y further.

Best Regards,

GIVENCHY
3, AVENUE GEORGE V, 75008 PARIS
TELEPHONE 225-92-60

Paris, October 16, 1978,

Mrs. Paige RENSE
Editor-in-Chief
Vice-President
ARCHITECTURAL DIGEST
5900 Wilshire Boulevard
LOS ANGELES,
California 90036
U.S.A.

Dear Mrs.Rense,

I have just received the beautifully binded book you so
about the apartments of some important people
_red to me, about how I have been touched and how
_d to tell you how I have been touched and how
beautiful present.
meet you in a near

This book is dedicated to Kenneth Noland (1924–2010), a great artist whose work is in museums and galleries throughout the world. He encouraged me and mentored me in ways I will never forget. And I will never forget the great man I will always love, Kenneth Noland.

ABOVE: Kenneth Noland in his studio with two paintings from his 1994 "Flows" series. RIGHT: Noland's *Fair*, 1960, in a Park Avenue apartment designed by Thad Hayes. March 1999

ARCHITECTURAL DIGEST

THE INTERNATIONAL MAGAZINE OF INTERIOR DESIGN AND ARCHITECTURE

MARCH 1999

ACKNOWLEDGMENTS

I would like to acknowledge with gratitude the writers and photographers who were essential throughout those creative years. Susan Mary Alsop, Gerald Clark, Nancy Collins, Brendan Gill, Joseph Giovannini, Paul Goldberger, Alex Gorlin, Elizabeth Lambert, Russell Lynes, Victoria Newhouse, Susan Sheehan, Jean Strouse, Judith Thurman, Marietta Tree, Jaime Ardiles-Arce, Robert Emmett Bright, Dick Busher, Billy Cunningham, Feliciano, Dan Forer, Derry Moore, Mary E. Nichols and Tony Soluri.

I would also like to acknowledge the extraordinary contributions of several members of my past *AD* staff in the years of inspiration and collaboration. James Huntington, my former photographer director, occupies a special place in my magazine heart. I could not have finished this without him. My thanks to Jim, with whom I worked at *Architectural Digest* for 30 years. It's not a casual thank-you; it's a deeply heartfelt thank-you for all his inspired efforts in completing this work. Another special few words go to Margaret Dunne, my former executive editor, for her invaluable help on this work from her office in Los Angeles. Margaret's knowledge of *Architectural Digest* past and present helped make this happen. Maile Pingel for her consistent enthusiasm and countless hours of editing, writing and researching, and for understanding the fundamentals of the magazine. James Munn for his assistance during the editing process. Copy editor Laurie Perry for her discerning eye.

Stephen Pascal who helped me with my years of initial manuscript. Thanks to the team at Rizzoli, especially Charles Miers and Anthony Petrillose, who had the foresight to see the great potential in this book, and to book designer Doug Turshen. To Christopher Donnellan, Matthew Barad, Marianne Brown and Samantha Vuignier for their assistance with the Condé Nast Archive. And to William Noland and Victoria Woodhull Cushing of the Kenneth Noland Foundation.

My thanks and greatest respect to the late, great S.I. Newhouse.

PHOTOGRAPHY CREDITS

Peter Aaron: 297

Jaime Ardiles-Arce: 66, 72, 92, 134-135, 136-137, 176, 177, 242, 244-245, 246-247, 248, 249, 316

Gordon Beall: 7, 299

Harry Benson: 203 (Kevin Costner)

Jeremiah O. Bragstad: 84, 85

Robert Emmett Bright: 86, 87, 96, 97, 154, 155

John Bryson: 198, 199

Richard Champion: 88-89, 90, 91, 94, 95, 98, 99, 100-101, 102, 103, 276-277

Clark: 16, 17

Copyright R.V.D.: 144-145

Courtesy Academy of Motion Picture Arts and Sciences/RKO Pictures: 196 (Jimmy Stewart)

Courtesy Academy of Motion Picture Arts and Sciences/MGM Collection/ Turner Entertainment Co.: 197

Billy Cunningham: 150-151, 162-163, 268-269, 270-271, 272, 273, 274, 318

Danforth-Tidmarsh: 42, 43

Lisl Dennis: 180, 181

Max Eckert: 30, 35, 38, 39, 40, 41, 82, 83

John Engstead: 33

Dan Forer: 168

Scott Frances: 230-231, 232, 233, 234-235, 279, 280-281, 285, 300-301, 316

Peter A. Freed: 196 (Helen Mirren)

Oberto Gili: 93

Green Studio, Ltd.: 44, 45

George D. Haight: 13

Marianne Haas: 128-129, 130-131

Hiller: 14

Pascal Hinous: 104, 105, 106, 107, 138, 139, 140-141

Yuichi Idaka: 46, 47

Bruce Katz: 298

Max Koot: 144 (portrait)

Robert C. Lautman: 284

Leland Lee: 48, 49, 50-51, 52, 53, 58, 58, 59, 60-61, 68-69, 70, 71

J. H. Maddocks: 21

Russell MacMasters: 108, 109, 110-111, 112, 113, 114-115

David O. Marlow: 217, 222-223, 278, 295

Norman McGrath: 190-191

Jim McHugh: 222-223 (Anjelica Huston portrait)

Derry Moore: 116, 117, 118-119, 120, 121, 122, 123, 124, 125, 126-127, 153, 164, 165, 178, 179, 184, 185, 188, 189, 224-225

Michael Moran: 290-291

Mary E. Nichols: 142, 172, 173, 174-175, 182, 183, 202 (top two photographs on the cover), 208, 209, 210-211, 212-213, 238-239, 240-241, 250, 251, 252-253, 254-255, 256,

257, 258, 259, 260-261, 262-263

Kenneth Noland: 8

Maynard L. Parker: 2, 22, 23, 24, 26, 27

Aditya Patankar: 226-227 (Shand with elephant)

Robert Reck: 226-227 (Seus home), 234-237

Louis Reens: 29

Euan Sarginson: 205, 206, 207

Durston Saylor: 166-167, 202 (bottom two photographs on cover), 215, 220, 221, 228-229, 264, 265, 266-267, 282-283, 288-89, 292-293, 296

Julius Shulman: 10, 18

Victor Skrebneski: 218-219

Tony Soluri: 160 ("Before & After" cover)

Tim Street-Porter: 156-157, 169 (right cover), 200

Jay Steffy: 73, 74, 75, 80, 81

Mott Studio: 12, 161

George R. Szanik: 19, 25, 54, 55, 56, 57

John Vaughan: 132, 133, 160 ("Country House" cover), 186-187, 192-193, 194-195

Peter Vitale: 146, 147, 287

Bruce Weber: 203 (Ricky and Ralph Lauren)

Charles S. White: 286

Herman How-Man Wong: 148-149

319